Buddy Rich's
Modern Interpretation of
Snare Drum
Rudiments

Order Number: AM 36419
International Standard Book Number: 0.8256.1003.6
Library of Congress Catalog Card Number: 43-10667

Exclusive Distributors:
Music Sales Corporation
257 Park Avenue South, New York, New York 10010 USA
Music Sales Limited
8/9 Frith Street, London W1V 5TZ England
Music Sales Pty. Limited
120 Rothschild Street, Rosebery, Sydney, NSW 2018, Australia

Printed in the United States of America by
Vicks Lithograph and Printing Corporation

Amsco Publications
New York/London/Sydney

Contents

Foreword

The circumstances surrounding the conception and publication of *Buddy Rich's Modern Interpretation Of Snare Drum Rudiments* were quite unusual. The thought of writing a drum book had never occurred to Mr. Rich, until he was suddenly inspired to do so through the vast number of inquiries he received from drum students and teachers from all parts of the country. He soon discovered, however, that his duties with the Tommy Dorsey organization would not allow him sufficient time to devote to writing a drum method, especially if the book called for early publication. Therefore, he immediately contacted his instructor and friend, Henry Adler — the well-known authority on percussion instruments — who agreed to collaborate with him in the compilation and preparation of such a work.

The result of the combined efforts of the Rich-Adler partnership is a book with all the fundamental material needed for an instructive drum method. In addition to the elementary principles of music, there are eighty-three lessons of exercises and rudiments, twenty-one reading exercises, ten exercises employing rudiments, forty-six advanced rhythmic studies and a list of the most frequently used musical terms. All of the material has been carefully graded as to difficulty.

Buddy Rich's Modern Interpretation of Snare Drum Rudiments not only differs from all other drum books, in that it contains a systematic course for the beginner, but it is also of great value to the teacher and professional who wishes to increase his knowledge of the rudiments.

When Mr. Rich approached us in reference to the publication of this work, we accepted it with a complete knowledge of his ability and genius in the drum world. We had perfect confidence that the book would prove to be an outstanding contribution to drum literature.

The Publishers

Introduction
by Tommy Dorsey

It is the opinion of the general public, especially of those who do not understand the importance and qualifications of a drummer, that he does not necessarily have to be a musician to play in a band or orchestra. They think that it is not necessary for a drummer to read music, that he is engaged merely to maintain *tempi,* and to beat a variety of rhythmical strokes as loudly as possible. This is false reasoning in regard to successful drummer.

In order to attain the height of his profession, a drummer must be as good a musician as any member of a band or orchestra. Not only is it important that he read music, but he must also have a solid background in the art of drumming; that is to say, he must be well versed in all of the rudiments. However, it might be well for me to state here that a drummer is often called upon to improvise a suitable part, because of the many faulty parts written by arrangers. Most of the drum parts, especially a great number of those in dance arrangements, are written as "guide" parts, leaving it entirely to the ingenuity of the player to use his own judgment.

It is true that a drummer can make more noise than any other member in the band, but an intelligent, capable drummer never goes to extremes in this respect; he carefully follows the dynamics, accents, etc., of the arrangement and style of the composition in bringing out the various necessary effects. At no time can a drummer do as he please, when it comes to playing louder than the music calls for; but his finesse in interpolating the various rudiments is always appreciated.

Most important of all, of course, is for a drummer to maintain a strict tempo. Nothing irritates a conductor more than for the drummer to play an irregular tempo — a tempo that constantly varies from fast to slow and vice versa.

The drummer who cannot read music, sooner or later, will be put through a test where he will be asked to read his part exactly as it is written or seek employment elsewhere. This is especially true of the drummer who plays in theatre, concert, school or symphony orchestras, or in concert bands.

Buddy Rich, the drummer supreme, has been with me for some time; and whether he is reading his drum part or creating one of his own, his handling of the drums and various traps shows the work of a genius.

Buddy Rich, even with his natural ability and talent, knew that, in order to become eminently successful, it would be necessary for him to gain the appropriate training. He had the foresight to engage a competent teacher, so that he would not, later on, have to overcome or undo any faulty habits.

In selecting Henry Adler to instruct him, Buddy Rich showed good judgment, for Mr. Adler has had great success in developing young drum students. In this connection, I also wish to say that Buddy Rich was extremely fortunate in securing Mr. Adler's assistance in the preparation of this drum method — a method which I feel sure will become a standard work in this field of instruction.

Selecting The Drum Sticks

When selecting the proper drum sticks, four extremely important features must be taken into consideration — *size, weight, levelness* and *balance.*

The *size* of the sticks is judged by the size of the student's hands; if his hands are large, he will naturally, need a larger pair of sticks than if his hands are small.

The *weight* of the sticks is determined by placing a stick in each hand and turning the wrists from side to side, several times. Then, if the sticks do not feel perfectly comfortable, as to the weight, other sticks should be tested, until the proper pair is found. It is also necessary that the sticks weigh the same; therefore, each stick should be weighed separately.

The *levelness* of the sticks is best tested by rolling them on the glass counter in the store. If, during this test, the sticks do not roll evenly, or have a tendency to wobble, they should be refused.

The center of *balance* should be a distance of about two-thirds from the knob (tip) of the stick, at the exact spot where it is held with the thumb and first finger. A good way to determine the center of balance is to hold the sticks in the correct manner and agitate the wrists with a motion similar to that used in executing the "bounce." *(See Lesson 33, p. 30)*

Various well-seasoned woods are used in the manufacture of drum sticks, but it is conceded by experts that hickory is the most satisfactory wood because of its durability and tone. The hardness of the wood denotes the tone. Naturally, a hard stick will have a sharper, crisper tone than a soft stick. A good hard stick has a twofold purpose; first, it is easier to handle and second, it gives a firmer stroke.

Drum sticks also come in a variety of stains, and with different shaped knobs (tips) and tapers, the choosing of which is a purely personal matter. None of these points, however, are as important as the size, the weight, the levelness and the balance.

After the proper pair of sticks has been selected, it is suggested that each stick be given a final test so as to insure a perfect match.

The Practice Pad

The best means of acquiring drum technique is to practice with the aid of a pad known as a *practice pad. (See illustration.)*

The practice pad is a small wooden contraption on top of which is cemented a rubber disk, or mat, forming the striking surface. In selecting the pad, particular attention should be paid to the quality of the rubber used for the disk which can be tested by tapping it with the drum sticks to see that the proper resiliency (bounce). If the rubber is soft or spongy, the sticks will not rebound quickly.

The purpose of a practice pad is threefold. First, the strokes are more pronounced than they are on a drum — every tap being clear and distinct. Second, it eliminates noise — the strokes being barely audible. Third, it is not as cumbersome as a drum.

The practice pad is manufactured in two different models: the *table* model and the *stand* model.

After learning the rudiments on a practice pad, the student may then apply them to the snare drum. He will, at first, discover a slight difference in the technique required for "plucking" the various strokes off the drum but, with a little practice, this difference can shortly be remedied.

In the following pages no further reference is made to the pad, because it is understood that the student will substitute the pad for the drum, at least, until he has gained perfect control of the sticks through accurate action of the hands, wrists and arms.

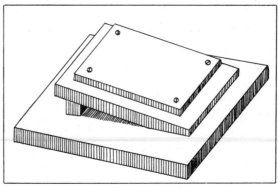

practice pad

Holding the Drum Sticks

To the novice, it would seem to be a comparatively easy matter to pick up a pair of drum sticks and mark time or beat out a simple rhythm. However, if the student aspires to become a proficient drummer, and reach the pinacle of success in this line of endeavor, it will be necessary for him to start at the beginning and learn to hold and manipulate the sticks correctly.

The correct manner of holding the sticks is explained in the following instructions.

How to Hold the Right – Hand Stick
(See Ill. 1)

Grasp the stick with the thumb and first finger of the right hand, at about two-thirds of the distance from the knob (tip) of the stick (the center of balance). The second, third and fourth fingers act in an auxiliary capacity as they aid in controlling the various movements of the stick. The palm of the hand is turned downward, upon striking the drum.

How to Hold the Left – Hand Stick
(See Ill. 2)

The left-hand stick is held at about two-thirds of the distance from the knob (tip) of the stick (the center of balance) in the crotch formed by the thumb and first finger. The second finger, acting as a guide, is placed on top of the stick. The third and fourth fingers, placed under the stick, act in an auxiliary capacity, while controlling the "swing" of the stick. The palm of the hand is turned toward the body, upon striking the drum.

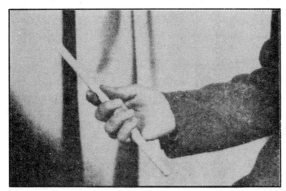

Illustration 1

Illustration 2

Hand, Wrist and Arm Action

After the student has learned to hold the sticks correctly, the next important procedure is to learn the correct movements of the hands, wrists and arms during actual playing.

Before striking the drum, the sticks are held with the points upward, as shown in illustrations 3 and 4. It will be noticed that the sticks are held in relative positions, with the hands raised slightly higher than the elbows. The wrists are not bent, and the arms, from the elbows to the hands, are straight. The elbows are close to the body, while the hands and forearms are away from the body.

In starting the exercises and rudiments, the position of the stick varies; sometimes the sticksis held up and, at other times it is held down. In any case, the movements of the hands, wrists and arms are always the same.

Taking each hand separately, the following instructions are given the student, in order to acquaint him with the correct method of manipulating the sticks.

Illustration 3

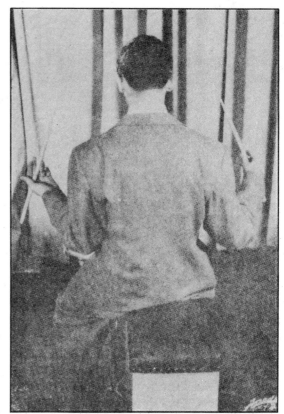

Illustration 4

The Right Hand

Start with the stick held as shown in illustration 3. Turn the wrist, while gradually bringing the forearm toward the drum. Upon striking the drum, see that the elbow is away from the body and that the hand is the same height as that of the elbow. *(See Ill. 5,)* After striking the drum, return the hand immediately to its original position.

The Left Hand

Start with the stick held as shown in illustration 3. Turn the wrist, while gradually bringing the forearm toward the drum. Upon striking the drum, see that the elbow is away from the body and that the hand is the same height as that of the elbow. *(See Ill. 6,)* After striking the drum, return the hand immediately to its original position.

All of the exercises and rudiments in this book call for the same hand, wrist and arm movements; the only variation is in the position of the stick when starting and ending an exercise or rudiment.

Illustration 5

Illustration 6

Elementary Principles of Music

NOTE: *In the following definitions and explanations of the various signs, symbols and characters used in music, there are a few which do not necessarily concern the snare drummer. They are included here, however, in the event the student might wish to increase his knowledge of music and perhaps, later on, take up the study of bells, xylophone, timpani, etc.*

Music is the effect produced by the combination of time and sound; or, in other words, of duration and pitch.

Music is written on a ladder-like arrangement called a *staff.* This staff consists of a series of five parallel horizontal lines, with their spaces.

Short auxiliary lines, called *leger lines*, may be added either above or below the staff, in order to extend its compass. The spaces between the leger lines are called *leger spaces.*

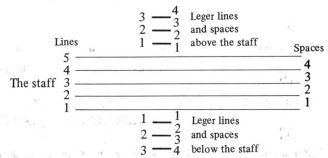

A vertical line drawn through the staff is called a *barline*. The strong or down beat always falls on the note immediately following a barline.

The space between two barlines is called a *measure*.

The completion of a musical phrase or sentence is indicate by a *double bar* — two light vertical lines. The end of a composition is indicated by a double bar, consisting of one light line and one heavy line. Dotted double bars, called *repeat marks,* indicate that the strain between two such marks is to be repeated.

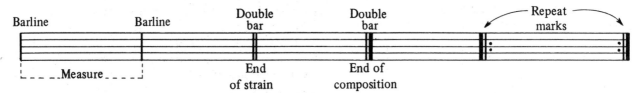

At the end of a strain, there sometimes occurs one or more *endings,* as follows:

The above endings might contain any number of measures. After repeating the strain, the second ending is to be substituted for the first ending.

The duration of rhythmical sound is represented by the shape of characters called *notes.* There are six kinds of notes in common use, as follows:

Notes

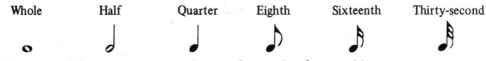

(The stems of the various notes may be turned upward or downward.)

Each note has its equivalent *rest* which represents silence, as follows:

Rests

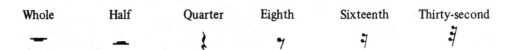

Chart Illustrating the Relative Value of Notes

A whole note
is equal to

2

half notes

4

quarter notes

8

eighth notes

16

sixteenth notes

32

thirty-second notes

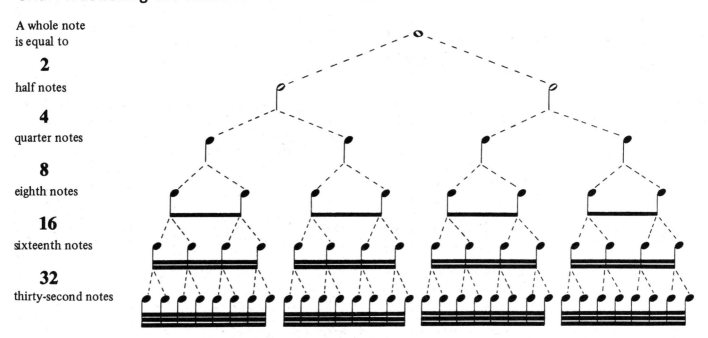

A dot (·) placed immediately after a note or rest increases the duration of that note or rest one-half.

Single
dotted notes

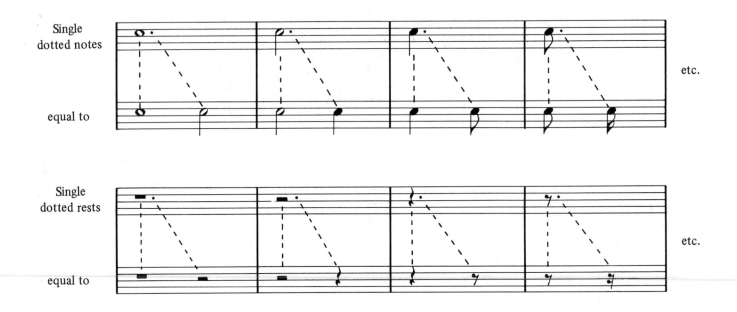

equal to

etc.

Single
dotted rests

equal to

etc.

Two dots (··) placed immediately after a note or rest increases the duration of that note or rest three-quarters.

Double
dotted notes

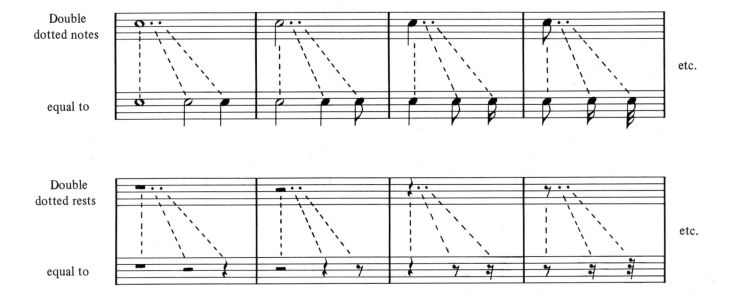

equal to

etc.

Double
dotted rests

equal to

etc.

The pitch of a tone is represented by a character called a *clef,* which is placed at the beginning of the staff. There are several kinds of clefs used in modern notation; however, in drum music, only two clefs are needed — the *treble* (𝄞) or G clef and the *bass* (𝄢) or F clef. The treble clef, which establishes the note G on the second line, is used for bells, xylophone, marimba, vibraphone, etc. The bass clef, which establishes the note F on the fourth line, is used for timpani, snare drum, bass drum, etc.

The degrees of the staff and the leger lines and spaces represent the pitch of various sounds which are named after the first seven letters of the alphabet — A,B,C,D,E,F,G. These letters are repeated as often necessary.

The note called *middle C* is placed on the first leger line *below* the staff in the treble clef and on the first leger line *above* the staff in the bass clef.

Names of Notes in the Treble Clef

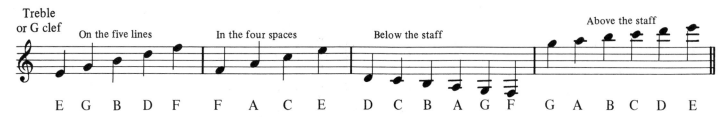

Treble or G clef	On the five lines				In the four spaces				Below the staff					Above the staff				
	E	G	B	D	F	F	A	C	E	D	C	B	A	G	F	G	A	B	C	D	E

Names of Notes in the Bass Clef

Bass or F clef	On the five lines				In the four spaces				Below the staff					Above the staff				
	G	B	D	F	A	A	C	E	G	F	E	D	C	B	A	B	C	D	E	F	G

The *time* or *tempo* in which a certain movement, or entire composition, is to be played, is indicated by two numerals (forming a fraction) placed at the beginning. This is called the *time signature.* The upper numeral (numerator) denotes the number of beats (counts) in each measure, while the lower numeral (denominator) denotes the kind of note, or rest, receiving one best, for example:

4 = Beats (counts) to a measure
4 = Note or rest receiving one beat (count)

Table of Time Signatures in General Use

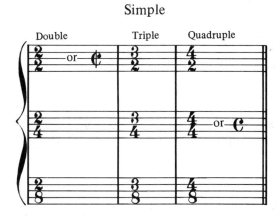

Simple

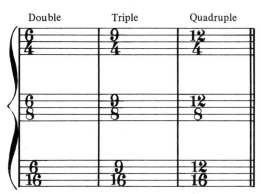

Compound

The *key* of a composition is indicated by characters called *sharps* and *flats* placed at the beginning of the staff, immediately following the clef. These signs of chromatic alteration are called the *key signature.* When no key signature appears after the clef, the composition is in the key of C major, or in its relative key of A minor.

All of the notes effected by the key signature are to be played sharp or flat, as the case may be.

When sharps and flats, not indicated in the key signature, and other signs such as *double sharps, double flats* and *naturals* appear throughout a composition, they are known as *accidentals.*

A sharp (♯) raises the note, before which it is placed, a half-tone.

A double sharp (𝄪) raises the note, before which it is placed, a whole tone.

A flat (♭) lowers the note, before which it is placed, a half-tone.

A double flat (♭♭) lowers the note, before which it is placed, a whole-tone.

A natural (♮) counteracts the effect of a sharp or flat and restores the note to its normal pitch.

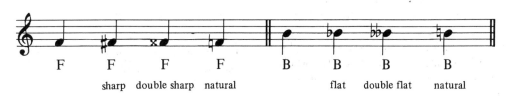

F	F	F	F	B	B	B	B
sharp	double sharp	natural		flat	double flat	natural	

Key Signatures (Treble Clef)

Major keys with sharps, and their relative minor keys.
(The key-note, or tonic, is given in each case.)

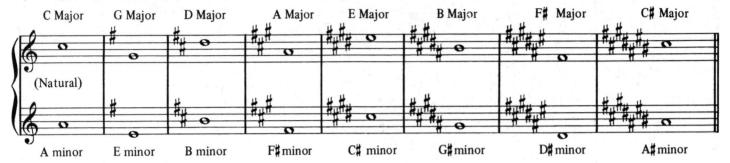

Key Signatures (Treble Clef)

Major keys with flats, and their relative minor keys.
(The key-note, or tonic, is given in each case.)

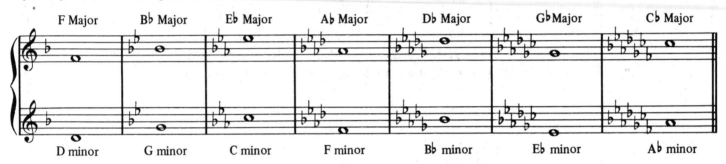

Key Signatures (Bass Clef)

Major keys with sharps, and their relative minor keys.
(The key-note, or tonic, is given in each case.)

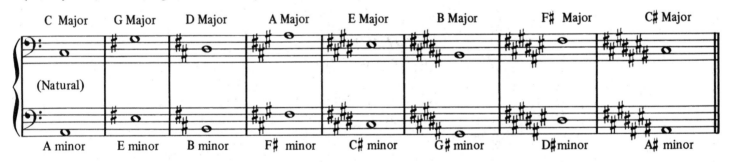

Key Signatures (Bass Clef)

Major keys with flats, and their relative minor keys.
(The key-note, or tonic, is given in each case.)

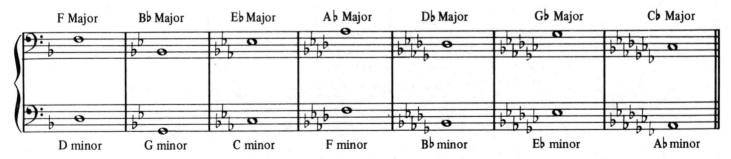

Notes grouped unevenly are indicated as follows:

 etc.

Abbreviations

This means to repeat the preceding measure.

This means to repeat the two preceding measures.

The word *bis,* meaning twice, is sometimes used to indicate the repetition of one or more measures.

Written

Played

Drum rolls are indicated in this manner:

 etc.

Dynamics
(Various Degrees of Power)

mp, mezzo piano

mp, mezzo piano means moderately soft.

p, piano means soft.

pp pianissimo means very soft.

ppp means as soft as possible.

mf, mezzo forte means moderately loud.

f, forte means loud.

ff, fortissimo means very loud.

fff means as loud as possible

sf or *sfz, sforzando* means forced — with sudden emphasis.

rf or *rfz, rinforzando* means to reinforce — with special emphasis.

fp, forte e subito piano means loud, then suddenly soft.

cresc., crescendo or ⟍ means increasing in loudness.

dim., diminuendo
decresc., decrescendo } or ⟋ means decreasing in loudness.

11

When a note is to be given special emphasis, a sign called an accent (> or ∧) is placed over or under it.

(Further study of accents will be found in Lession 3, p. 14)

Although a rather incongruous term, the word "fingering," in connection with drumming, refers to the right- and left-hand strokes, such as LRLL, RLRR, etc.

A sign called a *fermata* or *hold* (⌢), placed over or under a note, means that, at the conductor's or performer's pleasure, the counting ceases while the note is sustained beyond its normal duration. This is also true in the case of a rest having a fermata placed over or under it.

A short stop, or *pause,* is indicated by this sign, ‖ .

A curved line (⌢) connecting two notes alike in pitch is called a *tie.* The second note is not struck but its time-value is added to that of the first note.

A curved line (⌢) placed over or under two or more notes of various pitch is called a *slur,* which means that the notes so marked are to be played in a smooth and connected manner. This method of playing is called legato.

A note, over or under which a dot (·) is placed, is to be played in a short, crisp manner. This is called *ordinary staccato* playing. (This is called *ordinary staccato* playing.)

When a note is marked by a wedge-shaped stroke (⋎), the effect is increased. This is called the *full staccato.* When a curved line (slur) is placed over the staccato marks, the effect is decreased. This is called *mezzo staccato or half staccato.*

When a group of notes is to be played an *octave* (eight notes) higher than written, the abbreviation *8va* is placed over

the group. *Loco* means to play as written.

Lesson 1
Development of the Hands

In every drum rudiment, the important thing to remember is to make sure that the sticks are held correctly. In fact, before commencing any exercise, the student is advised to "check up," not only on the correct manner of holding the sticks, but also on the correct movement of the hands, arms and wrists.

Each of the following exercises is to be played in a very slow tempo, at first; later on, the tempo may gradually be increased, until a fairly rapid arte of speed has been attained. This, of course, must be done without interrupting the rhythm of the rudiment. As the speed increases, the student's forearms and hands will, naturally, get closer to the drum and still retain the same motions as those required for a slower tempo.

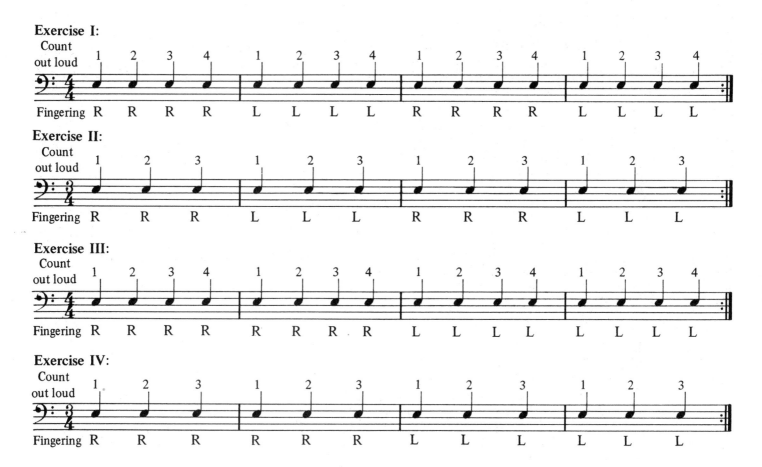

Lesson 2
Alternate Single Strokes

Alternate Single Strokes are very extensively used in both rudimental, as well as in original drumming. This method of playing Alternate Single Strokes is commonly referred to as "hand to hand" playing, and simply means that the hands alternate when striking the drum; each hand playing a single stroke at a time.

Instructions for Playing
Alternate Single Strokes

The correct position of the hands and arms, when playing Alternate Single Strokes, is as follows: *(See starting position shown in Illustration 3, p. 5.)*

First: Strike the drum with the right stick, and keep it down. *(See Illustration 5, p. 5.)*

Second: Strike the drum with the left stick and, at the same time, bring the right stick up to its original position. *(See Illustration 6, p. 6.)* Keep on repeating this process, first with the right hand, and then with the left hand, until the Alternate Single Strokes have been mastered.

In the beginning, the following exercises are to be played very slowly, the student bearing in mind the fact that the hands work in opposite directions, that is; when one hand is going toward the drum, the other hand is going away from the drum.

These exercises should be constantly repeated, until the student is positive that the hands move correctly.

After the exercises have been thoroughly learned in a slow tempo, the rate of speed may be increased.

Exercise I:

Exercise II:

The above exercises are given here for the purpose of preparing the student for the study of the Single Stroke Roll, which will be taken up later on, following the study of the Five, Seven and Nine Stroke Rolls.

By diligently practicing Alternate Single Strokes, the student will be able to acquire the proper movement of the hands and arms, which is extremely necessary in perfecting any rudiment.

Lesson 3
Accents

An accent is indicated by a certain symbol, or sign, denoting special emphasis. A note, over or under which an accent is placed, is to be played louder than the note not so marked.

There are two kinds of accents; the light, or weak (>), and the heavy, or strong (∧). A note marked with a heavy accent (∧) is to be played as forcefully as possible.

A finished performer on the drums will always make sure that he plays all of the unaccented notes in a normal way; which means that he plays them with an equal amount of volume. Then, when an accented note appears, he strikes it with more emphasis than he does the other notes.

The following exercises are to be played very slowly, at first, and in strict tempo. The accent must be perfected to such a degree that it will not interfere with the tempo of the music.

The hand motions, used in these exercises, are the same as those used for developing the hands. *(See Lesson 1, p. 13)* However, when playing an accented note, the arms and wrists are used with a "snapping of a whip" motion. This "snap" of the arms and wrists takes place during their normal movements. The student is advised against increasing the power of the accent by adding to the height of the stick, or by taking a longer swing with the arm. The stronger the wrists become (in the "snap"), the less the arms will have to move. The secret of executing an accent in a smooth, even manner, is to play it as close to the drum as possible, with a sudden "snap" of the wrist, but with only a slight arm motion.

When the student finds that he has perfected the system of playing an accent in a slow tempo, he may then gradually increase the speed, until he can play the exercises in a very rapid tempo.

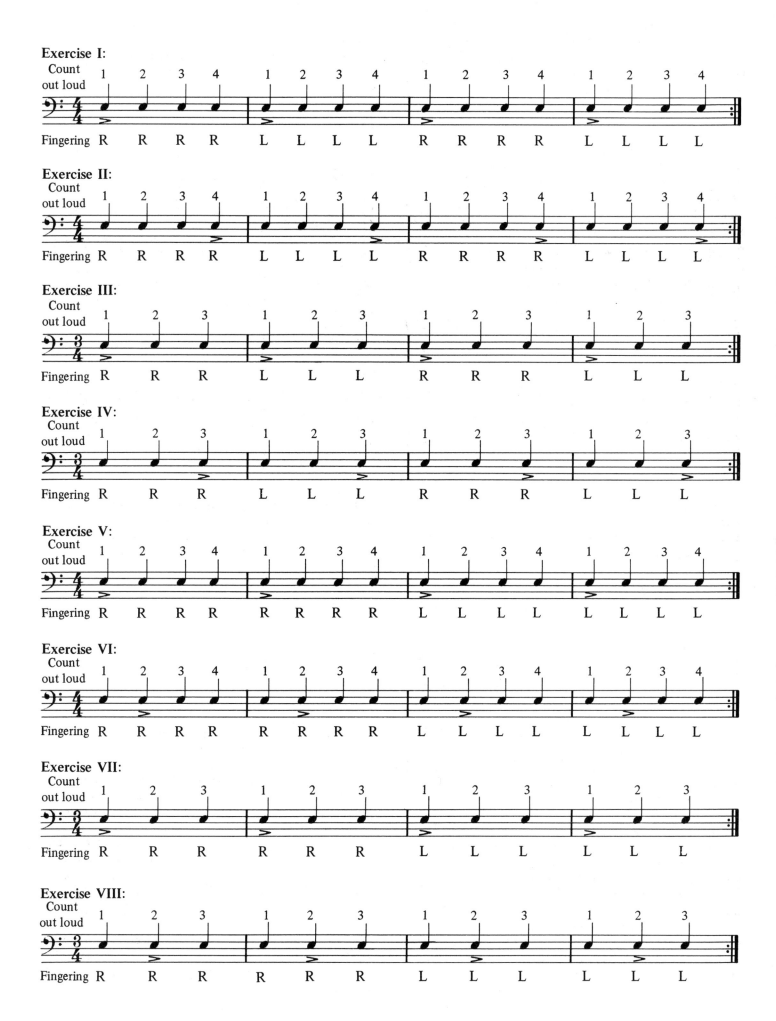

Lesson 4
The Three Stroke Ruff
with an accent on the third stroke

All short, Single Stroke Rolls are known as Ruffs. The rudiment, in this lesson, consists of three alternate strokes, the third of which is accented.

The rhythmic model of this rudiment, shown below, is written in common time (4/4). There are four beats to each measure, the fourth of which is a quarter rest. By playing this rudiment in strict tempo, slowly at first, and counting each beat out loud, the student will soon discover that the rudiment will automatically set itself into a definite tempo; especially as the rate of speed is increased.

Instructions for Playing the Three Stroke Ruff

At the start, both sticks must be up; that is, they must be raised above the drum. *(Ill. 3, p. 5.)* On the count of one,

bring the right stick down on the drum. *(Ill. 5, p. 6.)* Then, on the count of two, bring the left stick down and, at the same time, bring the right stick up. *(Ill. 6, p. 6.)* On the count of three, bring the right stick down with a "snap" of the wrist and arm, in order to produce the accent, and, at the same time, bring the left stick up. *(Ill. 5, p. 6.)* Then retain this position (right stick down and left stick up) on the count of four, which is a rest. Continue the exercise (rhythmic model) in the manner just explained, but take notice that the hands alternate on the first beat in each measure. Always pay strict attention to the fingering.

Rhythmic Model: Play slowly at first; increase speed gradually. Keep strict rhythm.

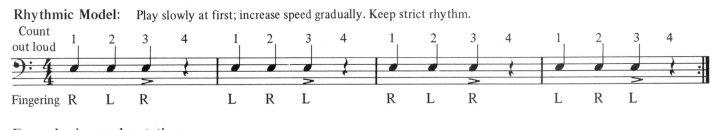

Examples in usual notation:

Grace notes are to be played very "close" to the large note.

Lesson 5
The Three Stroke Ruff
with an accent on the first stroke

This rudiment is almost identical to the one mentioned above in Lesson 4, except for the fact that the accent falls on the first stroke, instead of on the third stroke.

The preceding Three Stroke Ruff (Lesson 4) is the accepted version of this particular rudiment. By practicing the Three Stroke Ruff with the accent on the first stroke, instead of on

the third stroke, a much finer technique, as well as a firmer and broader knowledge of rhythmical beats, will be acquired.

The instructions given in Lesson 4 also apply to the following rhythmic model, with, however, the exception of the accent.

Rhythmic Model: **Play slowly** at first; increase speed gradually. Keep strict rhythm.

Examples in usual notation:

Lesson 6
Combination of the Two
Previous Three Stroke Ruffs

This lesson will give the student better control over each individual Three Stroke Ruff. It should be practiced very slowly, at first, gradually increasing the speed, and always bearing in mind the correct movements of the arms and wrists.

After this lesson has been perfected in a fairly rapid tempo, the student will experience little difficulty with a Three Stroke Ruff in any combination of accents.

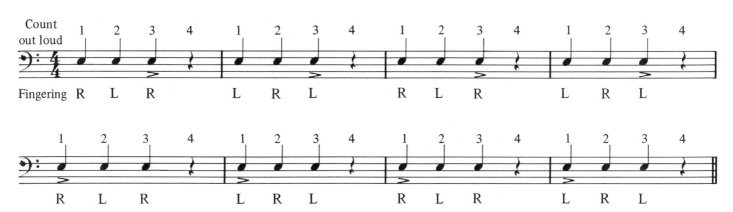

Lesson 7
Wrist Exercise for the Three
Stroke Ruff

This exercise, with the exception of the fingering, is the same as the one given in Lesson 6.

In the beginning, both sticks should be up. *(See Illustration 3, p. 5.)*

After striking the drum, the sticks must be returned to their original positions.

When starting slowly, the arms and wrists must be used in playing every stroke. Then, after a little speed has been acquired, the hands will gradually get closer to the drum, with the wrists doing most of the work.

17

Lesson 8
The Four Stroke Ruff
with an accent on the fourth stroke

This rudiment consists of four alternate strokes, with an accent on the fourth stroke. When the left hand stick begins the Ruff, the right hand stick plays the accented (fourth) stroke; and, when the right hand stick starts the Ruff, the left hand stick is given the accented (fourth) stroke. In other words, the hand that is down on the drum, remains down, after playing the accent, and starts the ensuing Ruff from this position.

The rhythmic model of this rudiment, shown below, is written in 6/8 time. There are six beats to each measure, the fifth and sixth of which are eighth rests.

It is advisable to start playing this Ruff in a slow tempo, at first, gradually increasing the speed, until the desired tempo is obtained.

By counting out loud and retaining a strict tempo, the student will, in a comparatively short time, acquire a perfect Four Stroke Ruff.

Illustrating the Four Stroke Ruff

Starting with the left hand:
First stroke, Ill. 6, p. 6
Second stroke, Ill. 5, p. 6
Third stroke, Ill. 6, p. 6
Fourth stroke, Ill. 5, p. 6

Fifth and sixth beats are rests. (Keep right hand down.)

Starting with the right hand:
First stroke, Ill. 5, p. 6
Second stroke, Ill. 6, p. 6
Third stroke, Ill. 5, p. 6
Fourth stroke, Ill. 6, p. 6

Rhythmic Model: Play slowly at first; increase speed gradually. Keep strict rhythm.

Examples in usual notation:

I

II

III

18

Lesson 9
The Four Stroke Ruff
with an accent on the first stroke

This rudiment is to be played in the same manner as the one given in Lesson, 5, p. 16, with the exception of the accent. The latter falls on the first stroke, instead of on the fourth stroke.

It is extremely important to count out loud.

The hand playing the fourth stroke of the Ruff must be kept down, ready to begin the Ruff following.

Rhythmic Model: Play slowly at first; increase speed gradually, Keep strict rhythm.

Examples in usual notation:

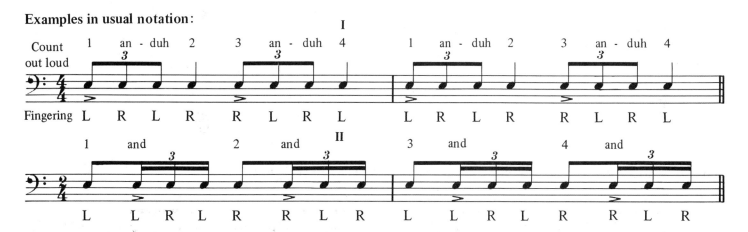

Lesson 10
Combination of the Two Previous Four Stroke Ruffs

This lesson is exactly what its caption implies. It will be noticed that, in each of the first four measures, the accent occurs on the fourth stroke of each Ruff; and, in each of the next four measures, the accent falls on the first stroke of each Ruff. Throughout the exercise, the hands alternate in playing the first stroke of the Ruffs.

Through careful practice, and by complying with the rules and instructions given previously, the student will, in a short space of time, master the Four Stroke Ruff, regardless of the accent.

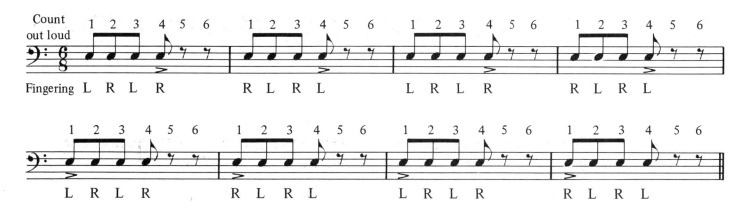

Lesson 11
Wrist Exercise for the Four Stroke Ruff

The instructions given for the wrist exercise in Lesson 7, p. 17 also apply to the wrist exercise for the Four Stroke Ruff, except for the accents and the difference in time.

Lesson 12
The Five Stroke Ruff

with an accent on the fifth stroke

This rudiment consists of five alternate strokes, with an accent on the fifth stroke.

The arm and hand motions, used for executing this Ruff, are the same as those used to execute the Three Stroke Ruff. Both of these Ruffs are practically alike; in fact, the only noticeable difference between them is that the Five Stroke Ruff contains two more strokes than the Three Stroke Ruff. In each Ruff, the accent occurs on the last stroke.

With the exception of the accents, the instructions given for the Three Stroke Ruff in Lesson 4, p. 16, are also applicable to the Five Stroke Ruff.

While increasing the speed from a slow tempo to a fast tempo, the correct motions of the hands and arms should not be sacrificed.

Rhythmic Model: Play slowly at first; increase speed gradually. Keep strict rhythm.

Examples in usual notation:

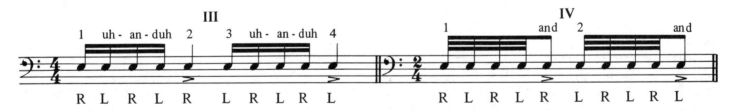

Lesson 13
The Five Stroke Ruff
with an accent on the first stroke

This rudiment is played in the same manner as the preceding Five Stroke Ruff, except for the difference in the accent.

The instructions given in Lesson 12, p. 20 also apply to the following rudiment.

Rhythmic Model:

Examples in usual notation:

Lesson 14
Combination of the Two Previous Five Stroke Ruffs

In each of the first four measures, of the following exercise, the accent occurs on the fifth stroke; while, in each of the next four measures, the accent falls on the first stroke.

When this exercise has been sufficiently practiced, the student will have little difficulty in playing any Five Stroke

Ruff, regardless of the accent.

The student is again advised to begin the exercise in a slow tempo, gradually increasing the speed, until a fairly rapid tempo has been reached. Counting out loud is also extremely important.

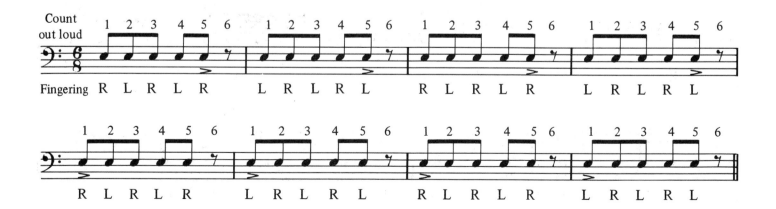

Lesson 15
The Five Stroke Roll
with an accent on the fifth stroke

The first four strokes of this rudiment are executed with each hand playing two strokes at a time; therefore, when playing the following rhythmic model, the first and second strokes are played with the right hand, the third and fourth strokes with the left hand, and the fifth (accented) stroke is played with the right hand, which should be raised so that it will be in position to start the next Five Stroke Roll. The latter is played in the same manner as the preceding Five Stroke Roll, except that it is begun with the left hand, instead of with the right hand.

Although the hands alternate by playing two strokes at a time, it can readily be seen that this is a "hand to hand" rudiment; however, the accented fifth stroke must not interfere with the position of the hands.

The count is the same as that of the foregoing Five Stroke Ruff.

It is advisable to master the Five Stroke Roll in a slow tempo, before attempting to play it rapidly.

Rhythmic Model:

Examples in usual notation:

Lesson 16
The Five Stroke Roll
with an accent on the first stroke

With the exception of the accent, this rudiment is played in the same manner as the preceding one in Lesson 15.

Rhythmic Model:

Examples in usual notation:

Lesson 17
Combination of the Two Previous Five Stroke Rolls

This lesson should be practiced slowly, until it is mastered; then, when this is accomplished, it will be easier to increase the rate of speed and still maintain clean rolls.

The accents should be carefully observed.

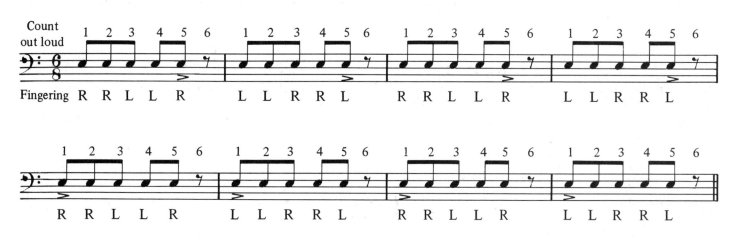

Lesson 18
Wrist Exercise for the Five Stroke Roll

This exercise, with the exception of the fingering, is the same as the one given in Lesson 17.

·The instructions given for the wrist exercise in Lesson 7, p. 17 also apply to this one.

Lesson 19
The Seven Stroke Ruff
with an accent on the seventh stroke

This rudiment consists of seven alternate strokes, with an accent on the seventh stroke. The latter, in 6/8 time, also happens to fall on the second major beat in the measure, which is the count of four.

In the following rhythmic model, in 6/8 time, the count is six to each measure. Each eighth note, or its equivalent in other notes or rests, is given one beat. However, in order to maintain an even tempo, the student is advised to count each half beat in this manner: 1 *and,* 2 *and,* 3 *and,* 4 *and,* 5 *and,* 6 *and,*

This rudiment should not be attempted in a rapid tempo, until it has been thoroughly practiced in slow and moderately fast tempos.

Rhythmic Model (A):

Rhythmic Model (B):

(This rhythmic model may also be used for all the succeeding Seven Stroke Rolls and Ruffs, except for the difference in fingering and accents.)

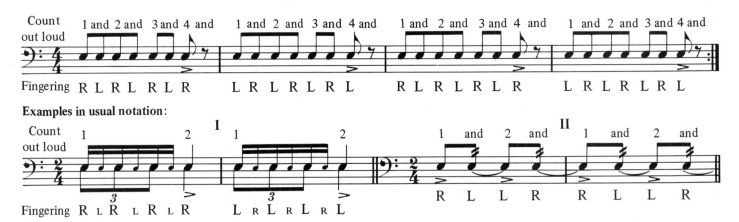

Lesson 20
The Seven Stroke Ruff
with an accent on the first stroke

The instructions given in Lesson 19 also apply to the following rudiment, except for the difference in the accent.

Rhythmic Model:

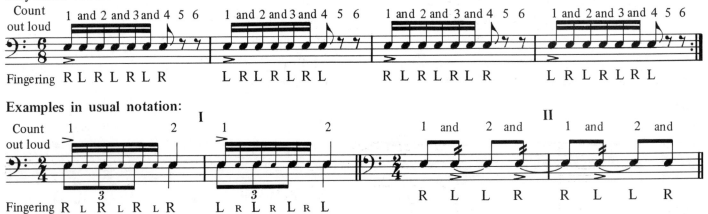

24

Lesson 21
Combination of the Two Previous Seven Stroke Ruffs

It is best to practice this exercise in a slow tempo, until it is well learned; after which, the rate of speed may gradually be increased.

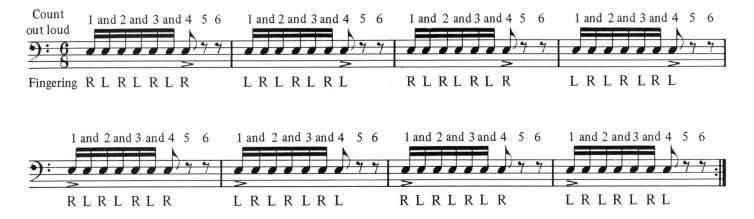

Lesson 22
The Seven Stroke Roll
with an accent on the seventh stroke

The rhythm of the Seven Stroke Ruff and Roll is similar to that of the Four Stroke Ruff.

The most appropriate manner in which to illustrate a Seven Stroke Ruff or Roll is to play it in 6/8 time. This will prevent the student from playing it incorrectly.

The hand ending a Seven Stroke Roll should be kept down, ready to begin the following Seven Stroke Roll—the same as in the Four Stroke Ruff.

Rhythmic Model:

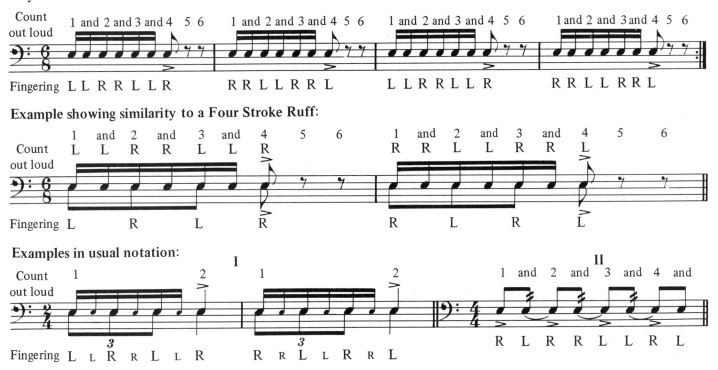

Example showing similarity to a Four Stroke Ruff:

Examples in usual notation:

Lesson 23
The Seven Stroke Roll
with an accent on the first stroke

This rudiment is played in the same manner as the preceding Seven Stroke Roll, except for the difference in the accent.

Rhythmic Model:

Examples in usual notation:

Lesson 24
Combination of the Two Previous Seven Stroke Rolls

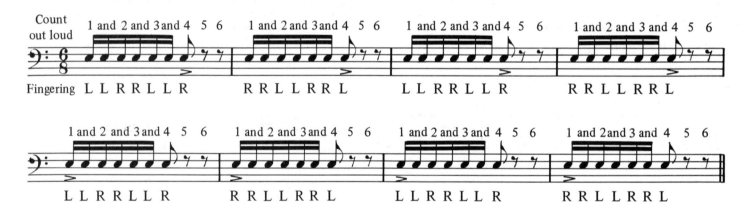

Lesson 25
Wrist Exercise for the Seven Stroke Rolls and Ruffs

The instructions given for the wrist exercise in Lesson 7, p. 17 also apply to this one.

Lesson 26
The Nine Stroke Ruff
with an accent on the ninth stroke

This rudiment is very similar to the Five Stroke Ruff.

It will be noticed that, in the rhythmic model, the accented ninth stroke is also the fifth beat of the measure.

In Example, I, given below, the Nine Stroke Ruff begins on the count *and,* following each beat; in which case, the accented ninth stroke falls on each beat.

Example II illustrates the abbreviated method of writing a Nine Stroke Ruff.

Rhythmic Model:

Example showing similarity to a Five Stroke Roll:

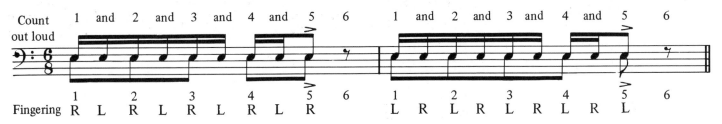

Examples in usual notation: As a rule, these are not played as Single Stroke Rolls.

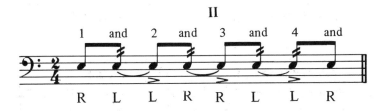

Lesson 27
The Nine Stroke Ruff
with an accent on the first stroke

The instructions given in Lesson 26 also apply to the following rhythmic model, except for the difference in the accent.

Rhythmic Model:

Examples in usual notation:

I

Count out loud: 1 and 2 and 1 and 2 and

Fingering: R L R L R L R L R L L R L R L R L R L R L R L R L R L R L R L L R

II

Count out loud: 1 and 2 and 3 and 4 and

R L L R R L L R

Lesson 28
Combination of the Two
Previous Nine Stroke Ruffs

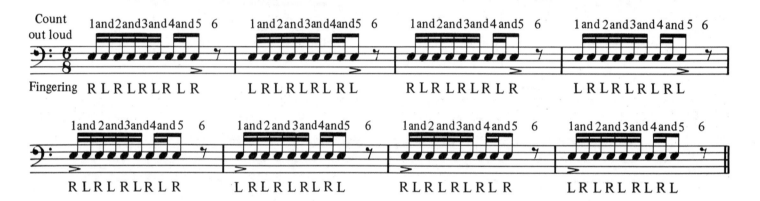

Count out loud: 1and2and3and4and5 6 | 1and2and3and4and5 6 | 1and2and3and4and5 6 | 1and2and3and4and5 6

Fingering: R L R L R L R L R | L R L R L R L R L | R L R L R L R L R | L R L R L R L R L

Count out loud: 1and2and3and4and5 6 | 1and2and3and4and5 6 | 1and2and3and4and5 6 | 1and2and3and4and5 6

Fingering: R L R L R L R L R | L R L R L R L R L | R L R L R L R L R | L R L R L R L R L

Lesson 29
The Nine Stroke Roll
with an accent on the ninth stroke

In this rudiment, the hands alternate by playing two strokes at a time; whereas, in the Nine Stroke Ruff, single strokes are alternated.

Rhythmic Model:

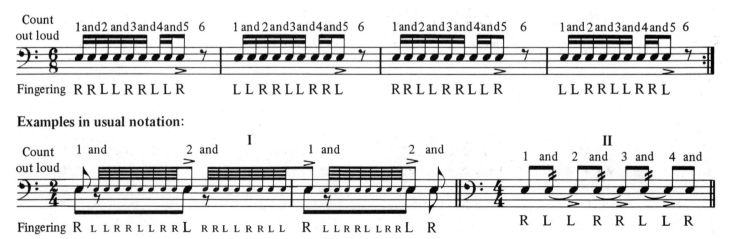

Count out loud: 1and2 and3and4and5 6 | 1 and 2 and3and4and5 6 | 1and2and3and4and5 6 | 1and2and3and4and5 6

Fingering: R R L L R R L L R | L L R R L L R R L | R R L L R R L L R | L L R R L L R R L

Examples in usual notation:

I **II**

Count out loud: 1 and 2 and 1 and 2 and | 1 and 2 and 3 and 4 and

Fingering: R L L R R L L R R L R R L L R R L L R L L R R L L R R L L R | R L L R R L L R

Lesson 30
The Nine Stroke Roll
with an accent on the first stroke

This rudiment is the same as the one given in Lesson 29, p. 28, except for the difference in the accent.

Rhythmic Model:

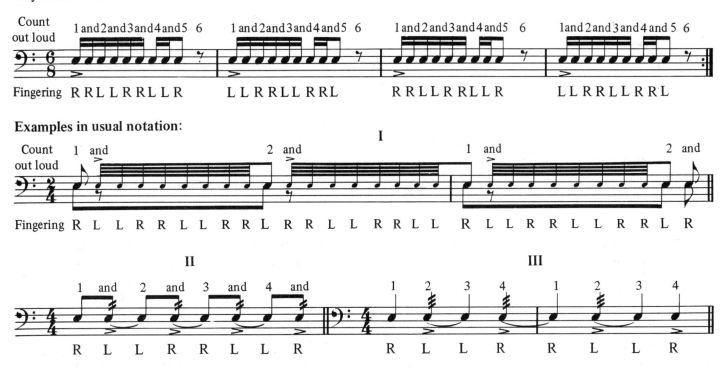

Examples in usual notation:

Lesson 31
Combination of the Two Previous Nine Stroke Rolls

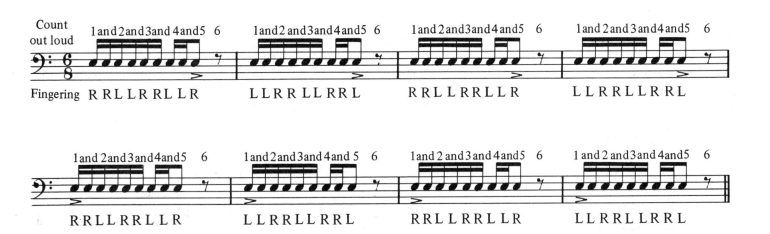

Lesson 32
Wrist Exercise for the Nine Stroke Rolls and Ruffs

The instructions for the wrist exercise given in Lesson 7, p. 17 also apply to this one.

Lesson 33
The Double Stroke Roll

This rudiment consists of the alternate playing of two strokes with each hand. It is commonly referred to as the "Daddy-Mammy" system for playing the Long (Double) Roll. Every stroke must be played with an equal amount of volume, and there must be no deviation in the rhythm.

After the student has acquired a certain amount of speed through the practice of this Roll, he will be ready to employ what is known as a "bounce." This will not only serve to increase the speed but it will also aid in relaxing the muscles of the hands, wrists and arms.

It will be noticed that, upon striking the drum with the stick, the latter has a tendency to rebound (bounce) of its own accord, although uncontrolled. The object is to control the "bounce" so that the student will decrease the amount of effort in his playing. During the "bounce" the hand and arm should be allowed to follow the upward action of the stick.

After practicing the "bounce" for a while, the student will gradually begin to coordinate the wrist and stick action; then, it will be only a matter of time when he will acquire perfect control of the "bounce."

When starting slowly, the wrist coordinates with each stroke; as the speed increases, the first right hand stroke is executed normally, and the second right hand stroke is "bounced," the fingers around the stick controlling the "bounce." This also applies to the left hand.

As the speed increases, the student must remember not to allow the second stroke of either hand to diminish in volume. In other words, every stroke, in a perfectly smooth Roll, must be made with an evenness of rhythm and an equal amount of volume.

The triplet rhythm exercise is a little more difficult to execute properly; it, therefore, will require more study, and ought not to be attempted until the Long Roll is thoroughly learned.

The rhythmic models, shown below, are self-explanatory. The student should be able to start a Roll with either hand; therefore, in order to insure this, he should practice it accordingly. *(Note fingering.)*

Rhythmic Model: (Long Roll)

Rhythmic Model: (Long Roll; Triplet Rhythm)

Examples in usual notation:

I

Count out loud   1   2   3   4   1   2   3   4   1   2   3   4   1   2   3   4

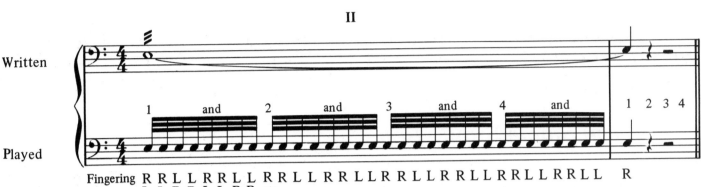

II

Written

Played

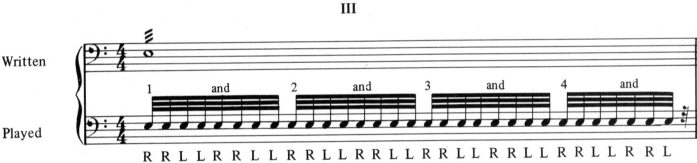

Fingering R R L L R R L L R R L L R R L L R R L L R R L L R R L L R
L L R R L L R R etc,

III

Written

Played

R R L L R R L L R R L L R R L L R R L L R R L L R R L L R L
L L R R L L L R R, etc.

IV

Written

Played

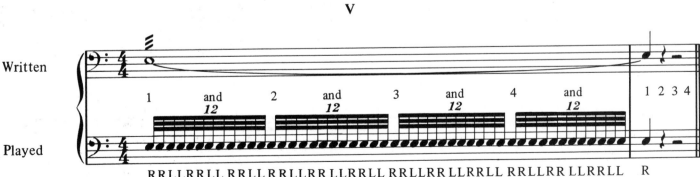

R R L L L R R L L L R R L L R R L L L R R L L L R R L L R
L L R R L L L, etc.

V

Written

Played

R R L L R R L L R R L L R R L L R R L L R R L L R R L L R R L L R R L L R R L L R R L L R
L L R R L L R R L L R R, etc.

Written

Played

Lesson 34
The Single Stroke Roll

Having already learned the correct arm and wrist motion of the Alternate Single Strokes, earlier in this book (Lesson 2, p. 13), the student is now prepared to take up the study of the Single Stroke Roll. The latter is merely a succession of Alternate Single Strokes, which are to be played as rapidly and as evenly as possible.

Both sets of fingering, indicated beneath the staff of the rhythmic model, should be practiced. The reason for this is, that the drummer must be proficient in starting any rudiment with either hand.

It is suggested that the student refrain from practicing the triplet rhythm exercise, until he has thoroughly mastered the Single Stroke Roll.

Rhythmic Model: (Single Stroke Roll)

Rhythmic Model: (Single Stroke Roll; Triplet Rhythm)

Examples in usual notation:

I

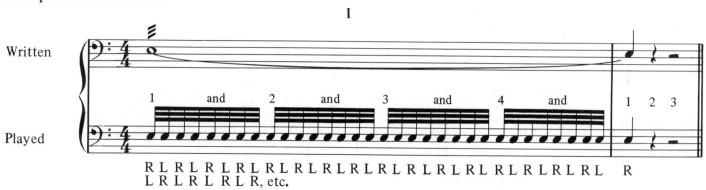

Written

Played

II

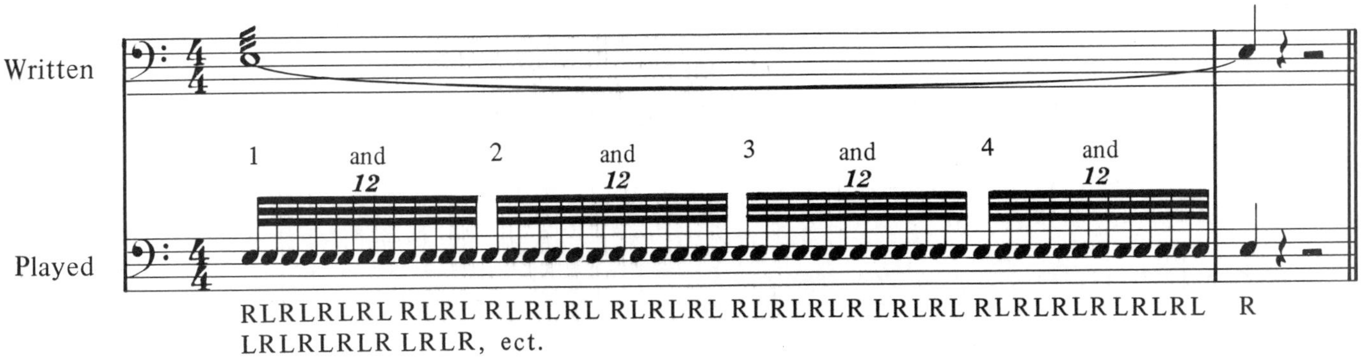
Written
Played
1 and 2 and 3 and 4 and
12 12 12 12
RLRLRLRL RLRL RLRLRL RLRLRL RLRLRLR LRLRL RLRLRLR LRLRL R
LRLRLRLR LRLR, ect.

Lesson 35
The Press Roll

This rudiment is executed with both sticks striking the drum simultaneously. The "bounce" of the sticks is controlled by "pressing" them on the drum.

The Press Roll should begin promptly on the beat, on which it is written, and care should be taken so that it does not continue to drag into the following beat.

The Press Roll is only used to produce a short, crisp Roll; however, dance drummers generally use it when executing quarter note Rolls in fast tempos. *(See Example 3, below.)* In any event, it is not advisable to employ the Press Roll, until both the Single and Double Stroke Rolls have been thoroughly practiced.

Examples in usual notation:

I

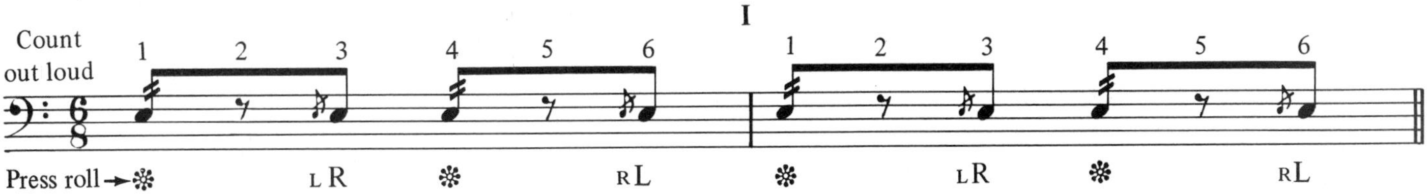
Count out loud
1 2 3 4 5 6 1 2 3 4 5 6
Press roll
LR RL LR RL

II

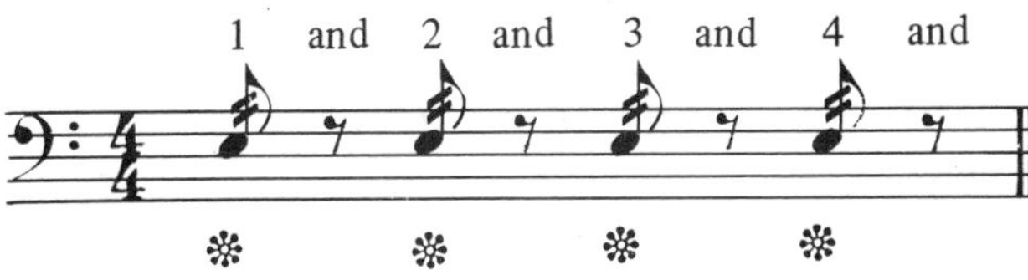
1 and 2 and 3 and 4 and

III

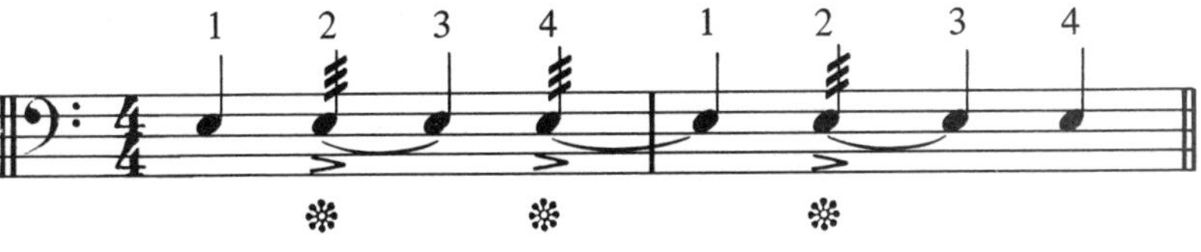
1 2 3 4 1 2 3 4

Lesson 36
The Single Paradiddle
(Stroke Paradiddle)

This rudiment combines two single strokes with one double stroke. The first stroke of the Single Paradiddle is accented by means of a natural down blow of the stick.

After completing the fourth stroke, the hand playing it should remain down; the other hand should be in an upward position, ready to begin the next Paradiddle.

Each stroke, with the exception of the first (accented) stroke, should be equal in volume.

ILLUSTRATING THE SINGLE PARADIDDLE

Starting with the right hand:
- First stroke, Ill. 5, p. 6
- Second stroke, Ill. 6, p. 6
- Third stroke, Ill. 5, p. 6
- Fourth stroke, Ill. 5, p. 6

Starting with the left hand:
- First stroke, Ill. 6, p. 6
- Second stroke, Ill. 5, p. 6
- Third stroke, Ill. 6, p. 6
- Fourth stroke, Ill. 6, p. 6

Lesson 37
The Double Paradiddle (A)
with two accents

This rudiment contains six strokes; four single alternate strokes, followed by a double stroke. The first and third strokes are accented.

The arm and wrist motions, used for executing the Double Paradiddle, are the same as those used for executing the Single Paradiddle.

Exercise I:

Exercise II:

Lesson 38
The Double Paradiddle (B)
with one accent

With the exception of the accent, which occurs on the first stroke only, this rudiment is the same as the one in Lesson 37.

Exercise I:

Exercise II:

Lesson 39
The Triple Paradiddle

This rudiment contains eight strokes; six single alternate strokes, followed by a double stroke. The accents occur on the first, third and fifth strokes.

The arm and wrist motions, used for executing this Paradiddle, are the same as those used for executing all of the previous Paradiddles.

Exercise I:

Exercise II:

Lesson 40
The Single Paradiddle

This rudiment, except for the added accent, is the same as the preceding Single Paradiddle in Lesson 36, p. 33. This lesson should also be practiced by accenting only the second stroke of the Paradiddle. The rhythmic effect, produced therefrom, will be well worth the extra time spent in practice.

Exercise I: **Exercise II:**

Lesson 41
The Double Paradiddle
with an accent on the first and fourth strokes

With the exception of the accents, this rudiment is the same as the Double Paradiddle (A) in Lesson 37, p. 34.

Exercise I: **Exercise II:**

Lesson 42
The Triple Paradiddle
with an accent on the first, third and sixth strokes

This rudiment is the same as the Triple Paradiddle in Lesson 39, p. 34. with the exception of the accents.

Exercise I: **Exercise II:**

Lesson 43
The Flam

This rudiment consists of a principle (large) note, preceded by a grace note.

In executing the Flam, the grace note is lightly tapped as "close" as possible to the principle (accented) note. However, it is advisable, in the beginning, to keep the two notes "open," gradually closing the grace note to the main note.

A right hand Flam is made by playing the grace note with the left hand, and the accented (large) note with the right hand. *(See Illustration 6, p. 6.)*

A left hand Flam is made by playing the grace note with the right hand, and the accented note with the left hand. *(See Illustration 5. p. 6.)*

The important points to remember are, that, when executing a right hand Flam, the left hand leads; and, when playing a left hand Flam, the right hand leads.

According to the fingering indicated in the rhythmic model, below, the right and left hand Flams alternate; while; in Example I, two sets of fingering are indicated — one for the left hand Flam, and the other for the right hand Flam.

The student is advised to thoroughly master the Flam, before attempting to play any beat containing it; otherwise, displeasing results are almost certain to follow.

Rhythmic Model:

Flam Exercises:

Lesson 44
The Single Flam Paradiddle
(Flamadiddle)

By placing a grace note in front of the first stroke of the Paradiddle, we have what is known as the Flam Paradiddle. The grace note, which is a light tap, is qucikly followed by an accented stroke; the latter, in turn, is followed by three normal taps.

Lesson 45
The Double Flam Paradiddle
(Flama - flamadiddle)

By placing a grace note just ahead of the first and third strokes of a Double Paradiddle, we have what is known as the Double Flam Paradiddle. In other words, this rudiment contains two Flams; whereas, the Single Flam Paradiddle has but one Flam.

Exercise I: Count out loud 1 2 3 4 5 6 | 1 2 3 4 5 6 — Fingering L R L L R L R R R L R R L R L L

Exercise II: Count out loud 1 and 2 and 3 and | 1 and 2 and 3 and — Fingering L R L L R L R R R L R R L R L L

Lesson 46
The Triple Flam Paradiddle
(Flama - flama - flamadiddle)

This rudiment contains three Flams. In reality, it is merely a Triple Paradiddle with the addition of a grace note placed in front of the first, third and fifth strokes.

Exercise I:

Count out loud 1 and 2 and 3 and 4 and | 1 and 2 and 3 and 4 and — Fingering L R L L R L L R L R R R L R R L R R L R L L

Exercise II:

Count out loud 1 uh - an - duh 2 uh - an - duh | 1 uh - an - duh 2 uh - an - duh — Fingering L R L L R L L R L R R R L R R L R R L R L L

Lesson 47
The Flam Tap

This rudiment is exactly what its name implies — a Flam followed by a tap.

The grace note is a very light tap and the next two notes are accented with equal volume.

The exercises in 2/4 and 6/8 tempos, shown below, will give the student sufficient practice in perfecting this rudiment.

Exercise I: Count out loud 1 and 2 and 1 and 2 and — Fingering L R R R L L L R R R L L

Exercise II: 1 2 3 4 5 6 | 1 2 3 4 5 6 — Fingering L R R R L L L R R R L L

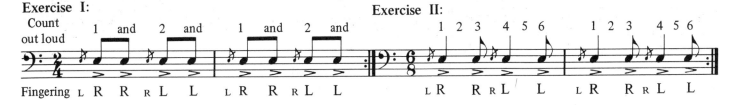

Lesson 48
The Flam Accent

This rudiment consists of a Flam, followed by two normal taps. The Flam Accent is most commonly written in 6/8 time.

However, it is also advisable for the student to practice the Flam Accent in the 2/4 tempo, as given in Exercise II.

Exercise I:

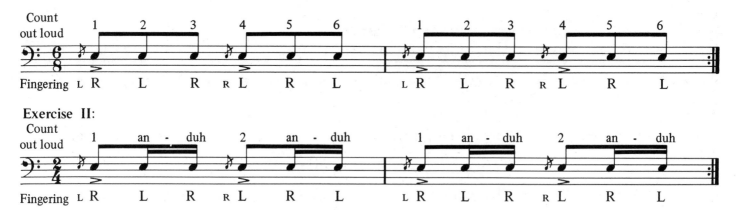

Exercise II:

Lesson 49
The Flamacue

In reality, the Flamacue is a Five Stroke Single Roll, with the first and fifth strokes "Flammed," and the second stroke accented. The Flams and accented note should have the same volume.

Exercise I:

Exercise II:

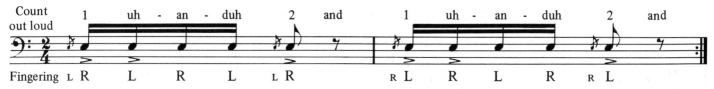

Lesson 50
The Half Drag (A)
with an accent on the third stroke

This rudiment consists of a double, normal stroke, followed by a single accented stroke. The rhythm of the Half Drag is similar to that of the Three Stroke Ruff, and should be practiced in the same manner.

The customary notation for the Half Drag is illustrated in Example II, shown on next page; which is two grace notes (double stroke) followed by the accented principle note. The grace note double stroke is to be "bounced," instead of "pressed," when speed is attained.

Rhythmic Model:

Examples in usual notation:

Lesson 51
The Half Drag (B)
with an accent on the first stroke

This is a "hand to hand" rudiment, which is chiefly used in slow or medium tempos. It is an exceptional rudiment for improving one's technique.

Rhythmic Model:

Example in usual notation:

Lesson 52
The Half Drag (C)
with an accent on the third stroke
(for rapid tempos)

This rudiment is more practical in a rapid tempo than the Half Drag (A) in Lesson 50, p. 38. This is due to the fact that the latter is played from "hand to hand" — a more difficult method of rapid execution.

Rhythmic Model:

Examples in usual notation:

Lesson 53
The Half Drag (D)
with an accent on the first stroke
(for rapid tempos)

In a lively tempo, this rudiment is easier for some drummers to play than the previous Half Drag (B) in Lesson 51, p. 39, because it is not played from "hand to hand." Both, however, should be mastered.

Rhythmic Model:

Examples in usual notation:

Lesson 54
The Single Drag

This rudiment consists of a Half Drag, followed by a single, alternated, accented stroke. In the rhythmic model, given below, the Half Drag occurs on the first and third beats in each measure.

Rhythmic Model:

Example in usual notation:

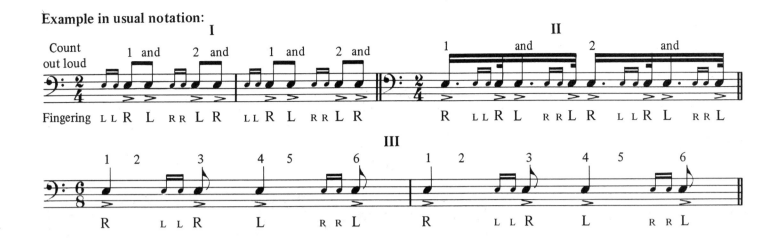

Lesson 55
The Full Drag

A Full Drag consists of a Half Drag, followed by a single, accented stroke; the latter is made with the same hand that completes the Half Drag. In the rhythmic model, given here, the Half Drag occurs on the first and third beats in each measure.

Rhythmic Model:

Examples in usual notation:

Lesson 56
The Double Drag

This rudiment consists of two Half Drags, the second of which is followed by a single, accented, alternate stroke. The student's attention is called to the fact that the two Half Drags, in succession, do not alternate.

The stick that concludes the second Drag, of the Double Drag, should remain down, so that it will be in position to start the following Double Drag.

Once again the student is cautioned to maintain a strict tempo, when practicing any rudiment. Even a slight deviation in tempo is not considered good drumming, and may lead into many difficulties later on.

Rhythmic Model:

Examples in usual notation:

Lesson 57
The Single Drag Paradiddle

This rudiment is a Paradiddle of which the first stroke is played as a Half Drag.

In order to determine the value of the two grace notes in their relation to the Paradiddle, this exercise should be practiced in a very uniform tempo.

Rhythmic Model:

Examples in usual notation:

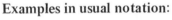

Lesson 58
The Double Drag
Paradiddle (A)
containing one Half Drag

By making the first stroke of a Double Paradiddle a Half Drag, we have what is known as a Double Drag Paradiddle.

Rhythmic Model:

Examples in usual notation:

Lesson 59
The Double Drag
Paradiddle (B)
containing two Half Drags

This rudiment is practically the same as the one in Lesson 58, except that the third stroke is also played as a Half Drag—making two Half Drags instead of one.

Rhythmic Model:

Examples in usual notation:

Lesson 60
The Triple Drag Paradiddle

This rudiment is merely a Triple Paradiddle with the first, third and fifth strokes played as Half Drags.

Rhythmic Model:

(Usual notation)

Another example in usual notation:

Lesson 61
The Three Stroke Ruff Single Paradiddle

By playing the first stroke of a Single Paradiddle as a Three Stroke Ruff, we produce a Three Stroke Ruff Single Paradiddle.

Before attempting any of the Ruff Paradiddles, the student must be thoroughly familiar with the Three Stroke Ruff and the Single, Double and Triple Paradiddles.

Rhythmic Model:

Examples in usual notation:

Lesson 62
The Three Stroke Ruff Double Paradiddle (A)

containing one Three Stroke Ruff

This rudiment is like a Double Paradiddle, except that a Three Stroke Ruff is substituted for the first stroke.

Rhythmic Model:

Examples in usual notation:

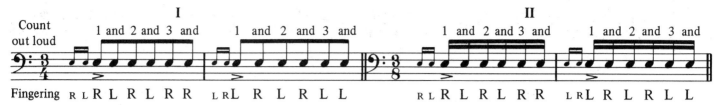

Lesson 63
The Three Stroke Ruff Double Paradiddle (B)
containing two Three Stroke Ruffs

This rudiment is the same as the one in Lesson 62, except that the third stroke is also played as a Three Stroke Ruff.

Rhythmic Model:

Examples in usual notation:

Lesson 64
The Three Stroke Ruff Triple Paradiddle

This rudiment is a Triple Paradiddle with the first, third and fifth strokes played as Three Stroke Ruffs.

Rhythmic Model:
(usual notation)

Another example in usual notation:

Lesson 65
The Four Stroke Ruff Single Paradiddle

By playing a Four Stroke Ruff, in place of the first stroke of a Single Paradiddle, the result will be a Four Stroke Ruff Single Paradiddle.

Rhythmic Model:

Examples in usual notation:

I

II

Lesson 66
The Four Stroke Ruff Double Paradiddle (A)
containing one Four Stroke Ruff

This rudiment is executed by playing the first stroke of a Double Paradiddle as a Four Stroke Ruff.

Rhythmic Model:

Lesson 67
The Four Stroke Ruff Double
Paradiddle (B)
containing two Four Stroke Ruffs

This rudiment is the same as the one in Lesson 66, except that the third stroke is also played as a Four Stroke Ruff.

Rhythmic Model:

Lesson 68
The Four Stroke Ruff Triple
Paradiddle

This rudiment is executed by substituting a Four Stroke Ruff for the first, third and fifth strokes of a Triple Paradiddle.

Rhythmic Model:
(usual notation)

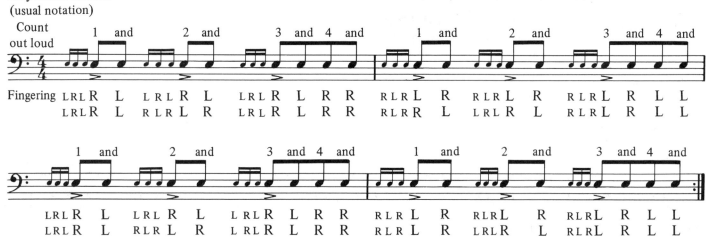

Lesson 69
The Single Ratamacue (A)
with an accent on the third stroke

This rudiment is executed like the Four Stroke Ruff, except that a Half Drag is substituted for the first stroke.

In the rhythmic model, all of the notes are equal in value (eighth notes). The purpose of this is to prevent the student from "pressing" the Drags, which might retard his efforts in acquiring clearness and speed in the execution of the rudiment.

In the two written examples, shown here, the first two strokes of the Ratamacue are to be played as grace notes. The

student should undertake great care not to "press" the grace notes, but to play them as closely as possible to the main (accented) note.

After the rhythmic model has been thoroughly learned, in the notation in which it is written, the student should then practice the examples in strict tempo, without interruption. By applying this method of practice to every Ratamacue, the student will have little trouble in mastering the rudiment.

Rhythmic Model:

Examples in usual notation:

Lesson 70
The Single Ratamacue (B)
with an accent on the third and sixth strokes

This rudiment is played in the same manner as the one in Lesson 69, except that the accent falls on the sixth stroke, instead of on the third stroke.

Rhythmic Model:

Examples in usual notation:

Lesson 71
The Double Ratamacue (A)
with an accent on the third and sixth strokes

By placing a Half Drag in front of a Single Ratamacue, the result will be a Double Ratamacue. This Rudiment has an accent on the third and sixth strokes.

Rhythmic Model:

Lesson 72
The Double Ratamacue (B)
with an accent on the third and ninth strokes

This rudiment is played exactly like the preceding one in Lesson 71, except that the accents occur on the third and ninth strokes, instead of on the third and sixth strokes.

Rhythmic Model:

Examples in usual notation:

Lesson 73
The Triple Ratamacue (A)
with an accent on the third, sixth and ninth strokes

By placing a Half Drag in front of a Double Ratamacue, we get a Triple Ratamacue.

The rhythmic model, shown below, clearly illustrates the exact manner in which this rudiment is to be practiced; and the written examples give its proper notation.

Rhythmic Model:

Examples in usual notation:

Lesson 74
The Triple Ratamacue (B)
with an accent on the third, sixth and twelfth strokes

Except for a slight difference in accents, this rudiment is played exactly like the preceding one in Lesson 73. p. 50

Rhythmic Model:

Example in usual notation:

Lesson 75
Combination of the Two Previous Single Ratamacues

In the rhythmic model, shown here, the accent falls on the third stroke in each on the first two Single Ratamacues, and on the sixth stroke in each of the third and fourth Single Ratamacues.

Rhythmic Model:

Example in usual notation:

Lesson 76
Combination of the Two Previous Double Ratamacues

In the rhythmic model given below, the accent falls on the third and sixth strokes in each of the first two Double Ratamacues, and on the third and ninth strokes in each of the remaining Ratamacues.

Rhythmic Model:

Example in usual notation:

Lesson 77
Combination of the Two Previous Triple Ratamacues

In the rhythmic model, given here, the accent falls on the third, sixth and ninth strokes in each of the first two Triple Retamacues, and on the third and ninth strokes in each of the remaining Ratamacues.

Rhythmic Model:

Example in usual notation:

Lesson 78
The Compound Stroke (A)
accenting the Half Drag

This rudiment is a combination of a Half Drag and a Three Stroke Ruff. The third (accented) stroke of the Half Drag is also the first stroke of this Three Stroke Ruff.

Rhythmic Model:

Example in usual notation:

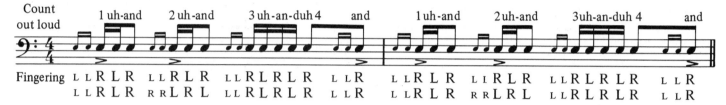

Lesson 79
The Compound Stroke (B)
accenting the Three Stroke Ruff

In this rudiment the accent falls on the fifth or last stroke of the Compound Stroke.

Rhythmic Model:

Examples in usual notation:

Lesson 80
Combination of the Two Previous Compound Strokes

In the following rhythmic mode, the first and second measures contain Compound Stroke (A), Lesson 78, while the third and fourth measures contain Compound Stroke (B), Lesson 79.

Rhythmic Model:

Examples in usual notation:

Lesson 81
The Compound Stroke (C)

This exercise is written in the conventional drum notation. The student should be able to play it in a fairly rapid tempo, carefully observing the accents.

Lesson 82
The Compound Stroke (D)

With the exception of the accents, the instructions given in Lesson 81 also apply to this one.

Lesson 83
Exercises in Triplets

A triplet is a group of three equal notes, ordinarily played in the time of one beat. When a triplet is played in the time of two beats, it is commonly known as a "drag" triplet, because it has a tendency to drag from one beat to another. Exercises 8, 9 and 10, in this lesson, are splendid examples of the "drag" triplet. While practicing these exercises (8, 9 and 10), it is advisable to mark time with the foot by beating four counts to each measure.

A simple way to remember the evenness with which a triplet is to be executed, is to pronounce the word "evenly," during its rendition. *(See Exercise 1, next page.)*

A triplet is easily recognized by the figure 3, which is placed either above or below the center note, as follows:

Each of the following triplet exercises is to be treated as an individual problem. Instead of playing them in a sort of slipshod fashion, it is best to master them one at a time.

Exercise I:

Play slowly, at first; increase speed gradually. Keep
strict rhythm. Count out loud. Observe fingering.
(The above refers to all exercises.)

Exercise II:

Exercise III:

Exercise IV:

Exercise V:

Exercise VI:

Exercise VII:

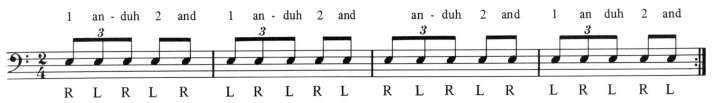

Exercise VIII:

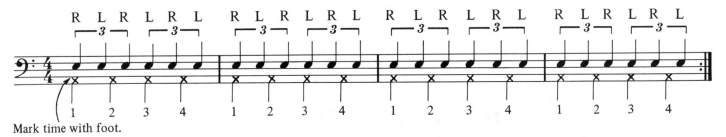

Mark time with foot.

Exercise IX:

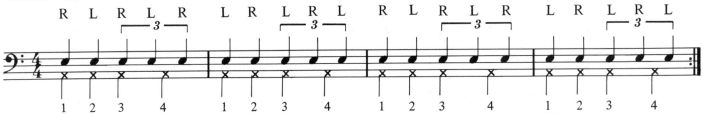

Exercise X:

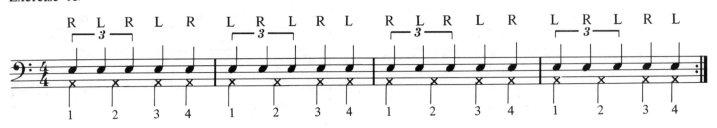

Reading Exercises

The following nineteen exercises are given here mainly for reading purposes. They are to be played in strict "hand to hand" style.

These exercises contain no involved or "tricky" rhythms, merely straight, simple rhythms.

It will be noticed that the counting is only indicated on the first line of each exercise; this method of counting, however, applies to all the lines in the exercise. The large encircled numerals, in the counting system, refer to the measures, and not necessarily to the beats.

Exercise I:

Exercise II:

Exercise IV:

Exercise V:

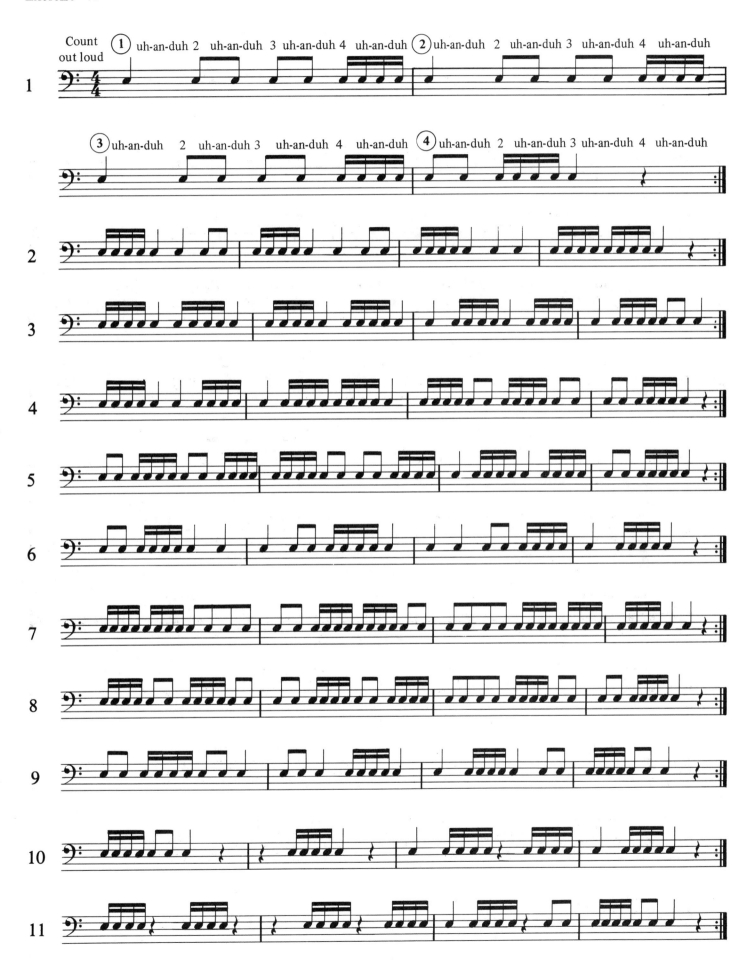

Exercise VI:

Exercise VII:

Exercise VIII:

This exercise illustrates the gradual development of a Long Roll, when played to a whole note, in four-four tempo.

A whole note Roll is generally written in this manner:

The three short lines, placed over the note, indicate that thirty-second notes are to be played to the time-value of the note. *(See line D.)* Sixteenth notes are indicated by placing two short lines over the note, in this manner: *(See line C.)* When eighth notes are to be played, one short line is placed over the note, in this manner: *(See line B.)*

The above abbreviations also apply to notes of other value, such as half notes and quarter notes. In rare cases, sixty-fourth note Rolls are played but this, of course, depends entirely upon the style and tempo of the composition.

In the following exercise, each line clearly illustrates how a whole note may be divided into notes of different value. The student is advised to practice these four lines in succession, without a pause, and to maintain a slow strict tempo throughout. Counting out loud is extremely essential.

In perfecting the Roll, this exercise is of great value.

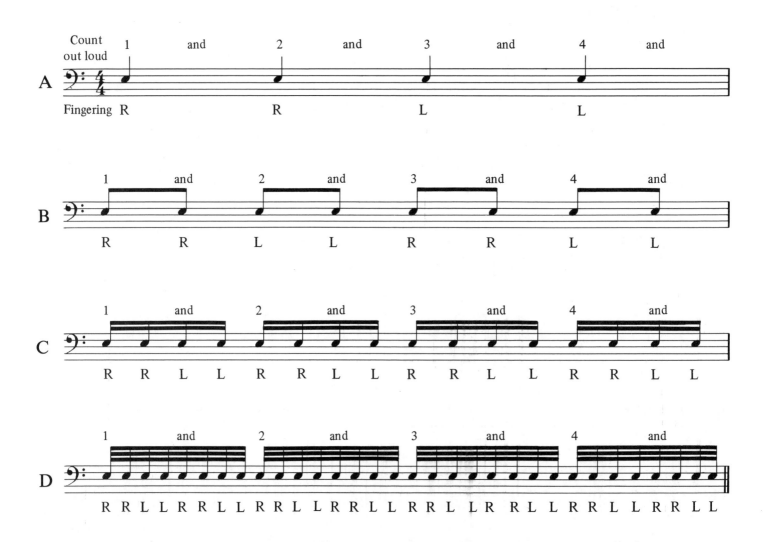

Exercise IX:

Exercise X:

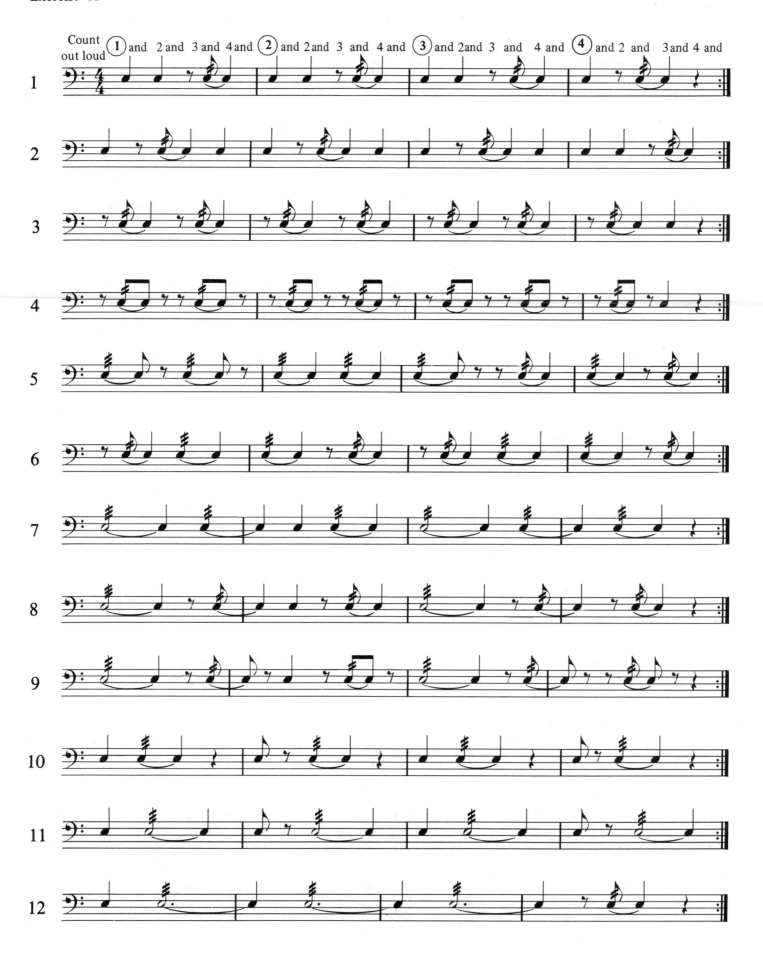

Exercise XI:

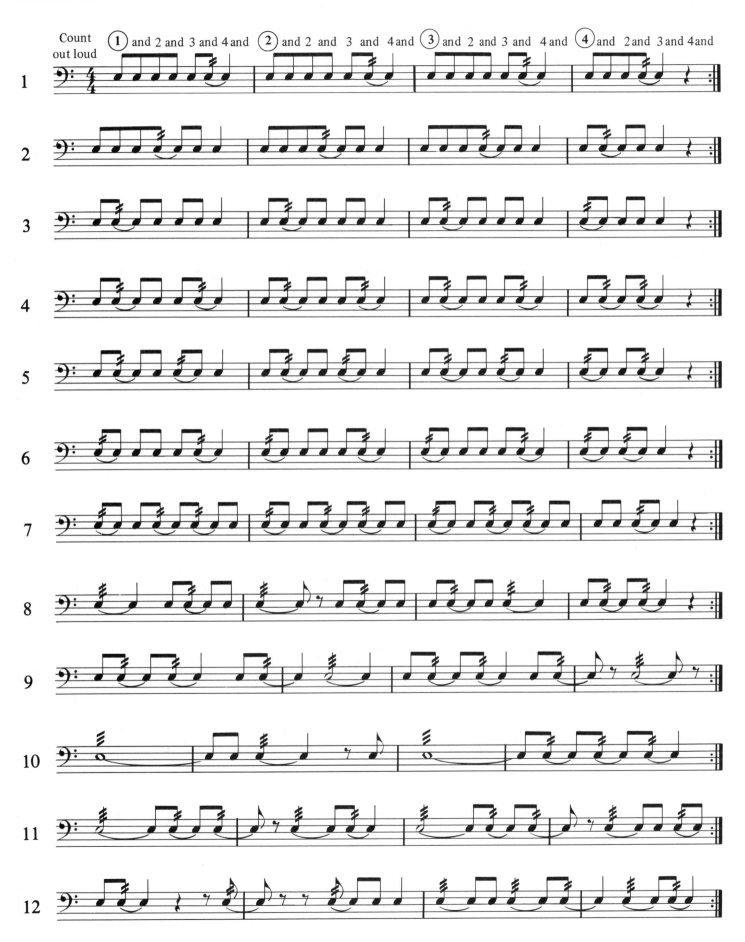

Exercise XIII:

Exercise XIV:

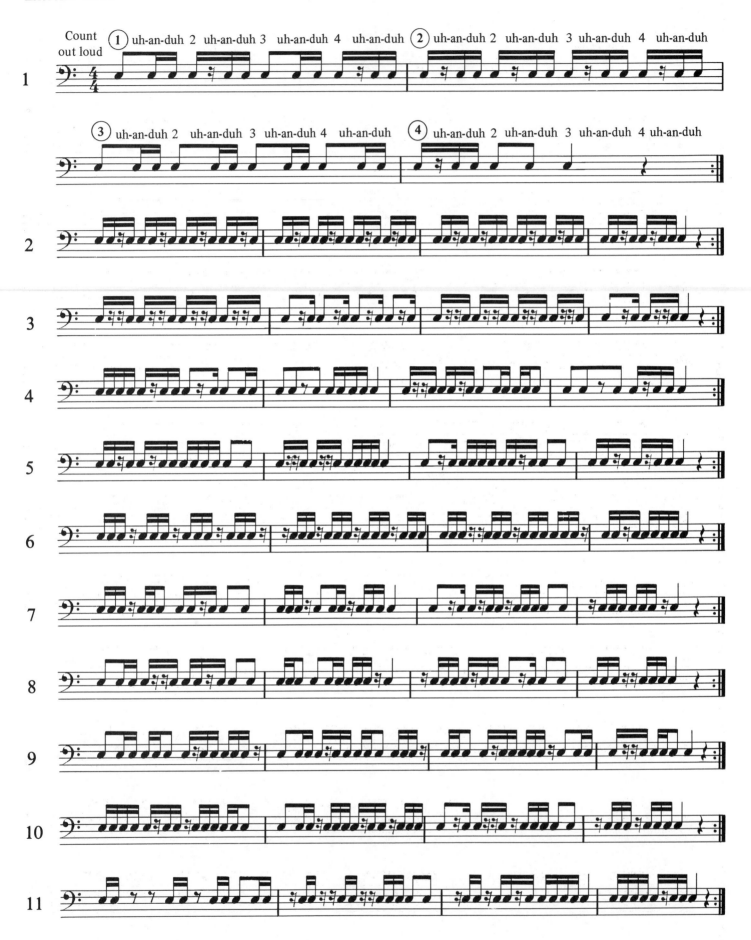

Exercise XV:

Exercise XVI:

Exercise XVII:

Exercise XVIII:

Exercise XIX:

Exercise XXI:

Explanatory Remarks
Concerning Exercies Employing Rudiments

The following ten exercises include all of the rudiments that are necessary in military drumming. The student is advised against attempting to practice any of these exercises, until he has first mastered all of the previous rudiments in this book.

As the rudiments employed in these exercises are not marked with any signs of identification, the student must be able to recognize them at sight, whenever he encounters them; and he should play them exactly as he has learned them. He will find this excellent practice in sight reading, which will offset any difficulties he might have later on, in the event he is called upon to play military drum parts.

Each line of these exercises should be treated as an individual problem. In fact, a good system to follow is to take one exercise at a time and play each line repeatedly, in a moderate tempo, until it is committed to memory; then play the entire exercise of ten lines from memory.

As a rule, the notation for military drum parts is slightly different from those of orchestra drum parts. In military music, it has always been the custom not to abbreviate the rudiments, especially the Stroke Rolls. In the latter, every stroke is written (usually in small notes) as played. *(See examples given below.)* However, it is a comparatively simple matter to learn to read either notation.

Excerpt from "The Three Camps"

Excerpt from "The Breakfast Call"

Excerpt from "The Dinner Call"

78

Exercises Employing Rudiments

Exercise I:

Exercise II:

Exercise III:

Exercise IV:

Exercise V:

Exercise VI:

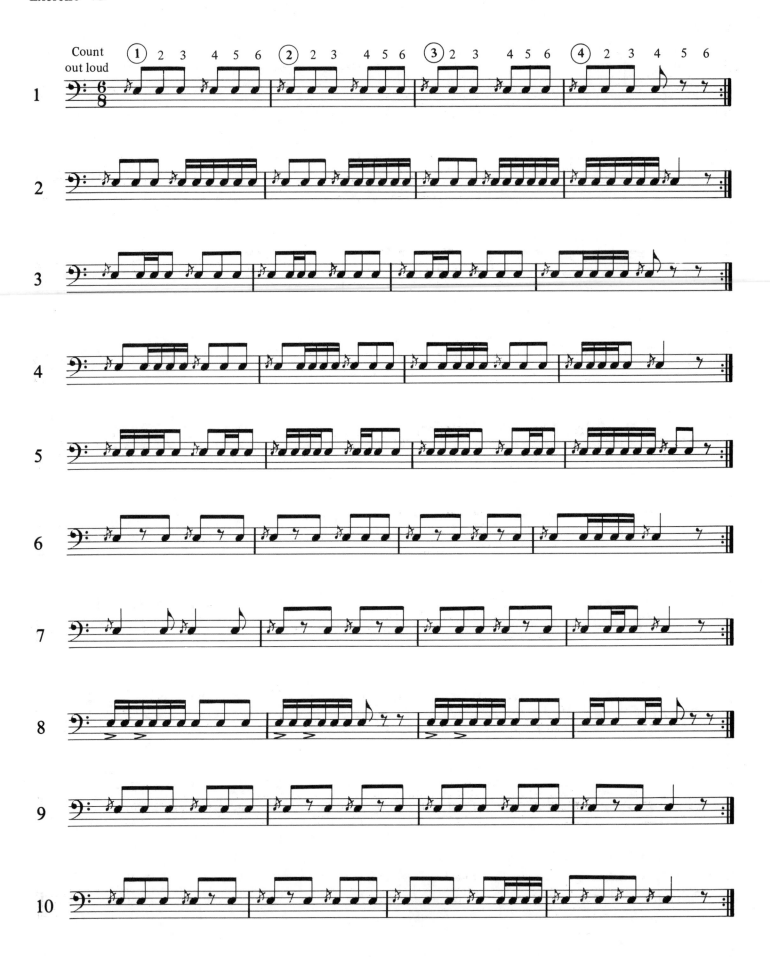

Exercise VII:

Exercise VIII:

Exercise IX:

Exercise X:

Buddy Rich in Action

Using the After Beat.

After all of the rudiments and exercises in this book have been thoroughly learned, the student may then practice them by holding the sticks timpani fashion, as shown above.

Advanced Rhythmic Studies

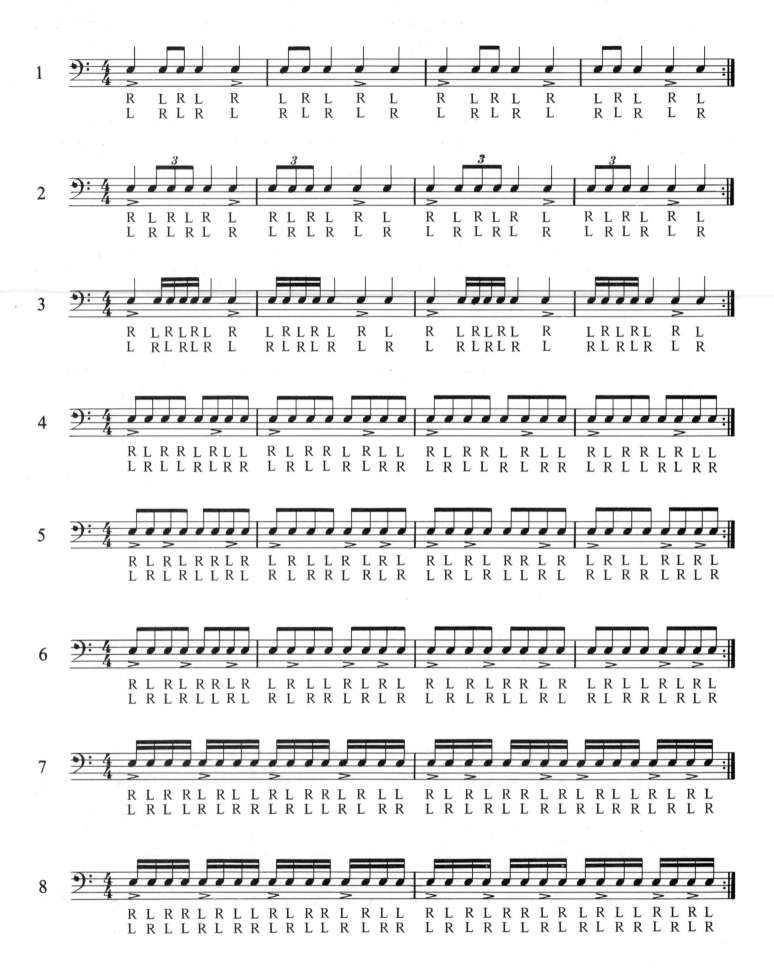

90

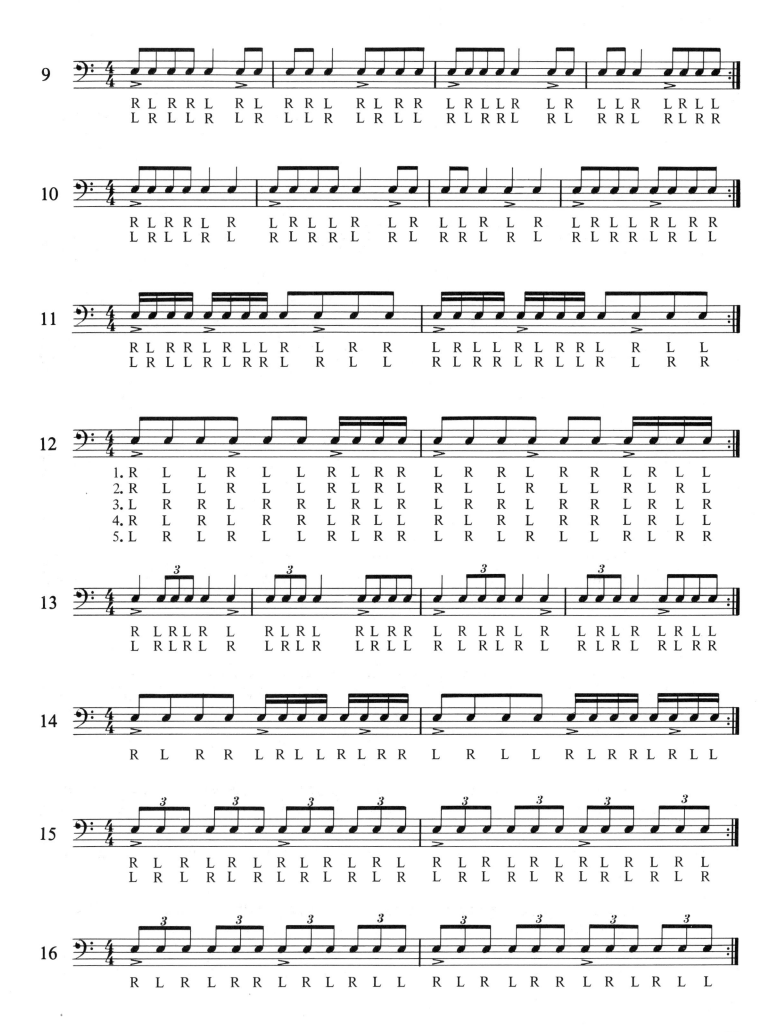

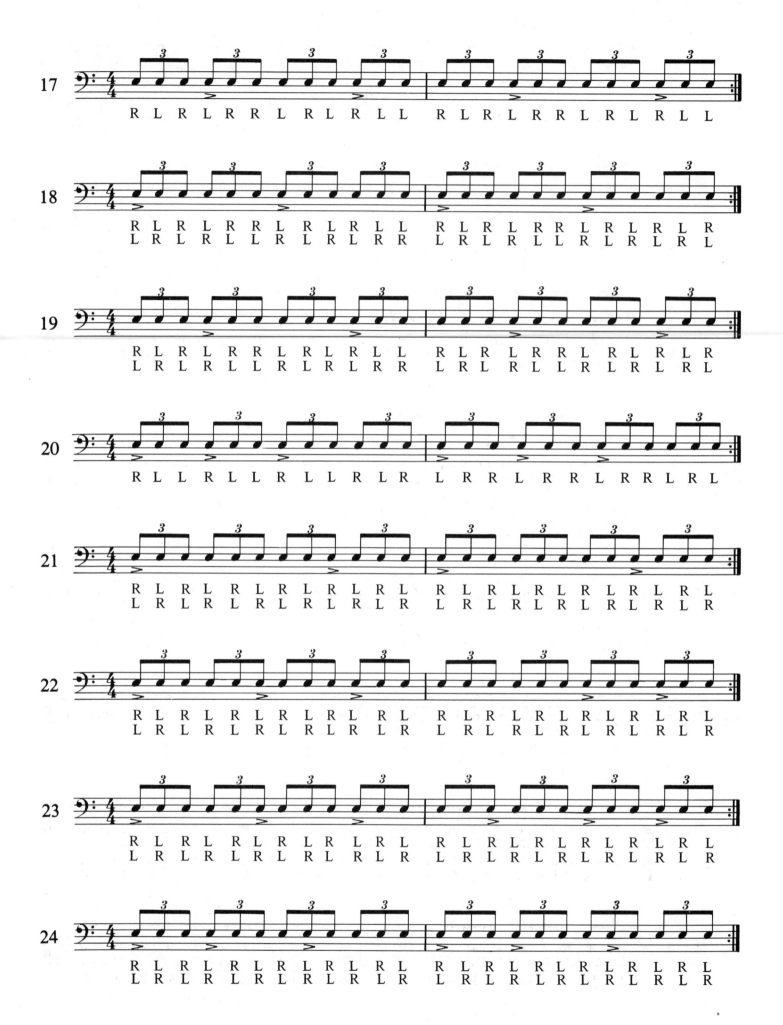

33

RLRLRLLRL RLRLRLLRL RLRLRLRLRL RLRLRLLRL
LRLRLRRLR LRLRLRRLR LRLRLRLRLR LRLRLRRLR

34

R L R L R L R L L   R L R L R L R R
L R L R L R L R R   L R L R L R L L

35

R L R L R L R L L   RLRRLRLLR L R R
L R L R L R L R R   LRLLRLRRL R L L

36

R L R L R R L R   L R L L R L R L
L R L R L L R L   R L R R L R L R

37

1.R L R L R R L R   L R L L RLRRLRLL
2.L R L R L L R L   R L R R LRLLRLRR
3.R L R L R R L R   L R L L RLRLRLRL
4.L R L R L L R L   R L R R LRLRLRLR

38

RLRRLRLLRLRLRLRL RLRRLRLLRLRLRLRL
LRLLRLRRLRLRLRLR LRLLRLRRLRLRLRLR

39

RLRLRLRLRLRLRLRL RLRLRLRLRLR L R R
LRLRLRLRLRLRLRLR LRLRLRLRLRL R L L

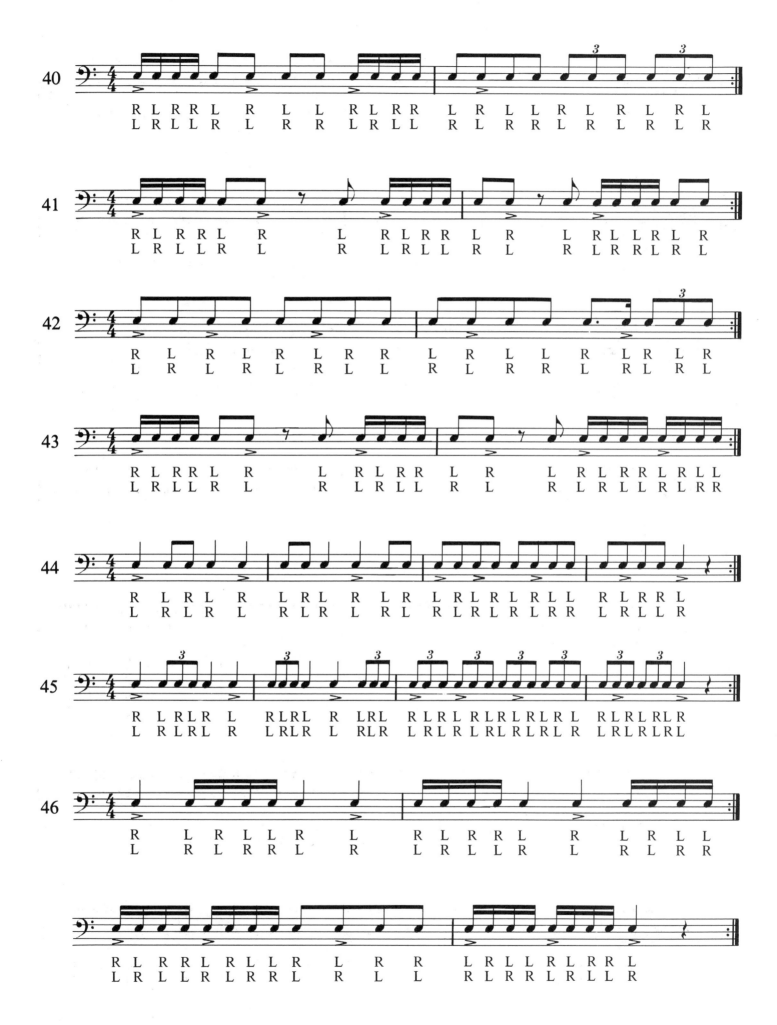

Musical Terms

Accelerando — accelerating, growing faster.

Adagio — slow, leisurely.

Ad libitum (ad lib.) — at will, at pleasure.

Affettuoso — with emotion.

Agitato — agitated.

Allargando — growing broader.

Allegretto — moderately fast; slower than *allegro*.

Allegro — brisk, lively.

Amoroso — amorous, loving.

Andante — moderately slow.

Andantino — slower than *andante*.

Animato — animated.

Assai — very; used to intensify a tempo mark, as *allegro assai* — very fast.

Ben — well; as *ben marcato* — well marked.

Brillante — brilliant.

Brio, con — with fire.

Cantabile — in a singing style.

D.C. (da capo) — from the beginning.

D.C. al Coda — from the beginning to the coda.

Dolce — sweet.

D.S. (dal segno) — from the sign 𝄋

D.S. al fine — from the sign (𝄋) to the word *fine*.

Energico — energetic.

Espressione, con — with expression.

Espressivo — expressive.

Fine — end.

Forza, con — with force.

Furioso — furious, passionate.

Grandioso — grand, pompous.

Grave — grave, heavy.

Grazioso — graceful.

Gusto, con — with taste.

Larghetto — rather broad, slightly faster than *largo*.

Largo — large, broad.

Lento — slow.

L'Istesso tempo — the same time.

Ma — but; as *allegro, ma non troppo* — fast, but not too much so.

Maestoso — majestic.

Marcato — marked.

Meno mosso — less speed.

Mesto — melancholy.

Moderato — moderate; at a moderate pace.

Molto — much; as *molto allegro* — very fast.

Morendo — dying away, growing softer and softer.

Moto, con — with motion.

Non troppo — not too much.

Pesante — heavy, ponderous.

Piacere, a — same as *ad lib*.

Più mosso — more speed.

Poco — little; *poco a poco* — little by little.

Pomposo — pompous, dignified.

Prestissimo — very quick.

Presto — quick.

Quasi — as if, like.

Rallentando (rall.) — gradually slackening the pace.

Ritardando (rit.) — retarding.

Ritenuto — holding back.

Scherzando — in a playful style.

Segue — follows.

Semplice — simple, plain.

Sempre — always; as *sempre staccato*.

Smorzando — fading away.

Sostenuto — sustained.

Spirito, con — with spirit.

Stringendo — hurrying.

Subito — suddenly.

Tempo — time; *a tempo* — return to the original tempo.

Tenerezza, con — with tenderness.

Tenuto — held; a note so marked should be given its full time-value.

Vivace — vivacious, lively.

Vigoroso — vigorous.

Volti — turn over; *volti subito (V.S.)* — turn over quickly.